SEAG
Practice Paper

Set A: Paper 1

For the Entrance Assessment / Transfer Test

Read the following:

Do not start the test until you are told to do so.

1. At the start of this paper, there is a Practice Test, which has 5 English questions and 5 Maths questions. These questions will not be marked and are not timed.

2. The Main Test has 2 sections, English and Maths. There are 28 questions in each section. You have one hour to answer all the questions.

3. You should mark your answer to each question in pencil on the separate answer sheet. If you make a mistake, rub it out and mark your new answer clearly.

4. You should do any working out on a separate piece of paper.

English — Practice Test

The sentence below contains either **one** punctuation mistake or **no** punctuation mistake. Work out which group of words in the sentence contains a mistake and mark the letter on your answer sheet. **Mark N if there is no mistake.**

P1   For our trip to madrid, I'll have to remind Gemma to pack lots of clothes.

        A   B   C   D   N

Choose the **best** word to complete the sentence. The sentence needs to make sense and be written in correct English. Pick **one** of the five options and mark the letter on your answer sheet.

P2   The students made a present for **many them their they mine** teacher.

        A   B   C   D   E

The sentence below contains either **one** spelling mistake or **no** spelling mistake. Work out which group of words in the sentence contains a mistake and mark the letter on your answer sheet. **Mark N if there is no mistake.**

P3   The intelligent detective found the suspect's behaviour extremely suspitious.

        A   B   C   D   N

The Unlucky Day

Ryan couldn't believe his bad luck. First, he'd slept through his alarm and had to get ready in a hurry. Then his dad's car wouldn't start, meaning he would have to get the bus to school. And finally, as he ran towards the empty bus stop, he realised that he had arrived minutes too late.

5   As Ryan stood alone at the bus stop waiting for the next bus to arrive, he began to feel like he'd been cursed. He stared furiously ahead as the minutes passed by and no bus turned up.

Eventually, he started to calm down. He reassured himself that things couldn't possibly get worse, and that the rest of the day would surely improve. Just as the scowl on his face

10   was replaced by a relaxed smile, he spotted a rain cloud out of the corner of his eye...

For this question, choose **one** answer from the options below
and mark its letter on your answer sheet.

P4   **Why does Ryan have to get the bus to school?**

   A Because he slept through his alarm.
   B Because he has been cursed.
   C Because his dad's car wouldn't start.
   D Because he got ready in a hurry.
   E Because it's about to rain.

For this question, you have to **write your answer** in the box on your answer sheet (box P5).

P5   **Which one word from the text means 'angrily'?**

End of English Practice Questions. Do not go on until you are told to.

Maths — Practice Test

Now try practice questions P6 to P10.
Read each question carefully before attempting to answer it.

P6 The table shows the birthdays of six children.

Name	Date
Cormac	1st February
Amani	22nd January
Maria	8th January
Liam	27th January
Rowan	17th January
Elise	31st January

Whose birthday is 5 days after Amani's?

A Cormac **B** Maria **C** Liam **D** Rowan **E** Elise

P7 The Salah family record how many hikes they go on each month.
Their numbers are shown in this chart.

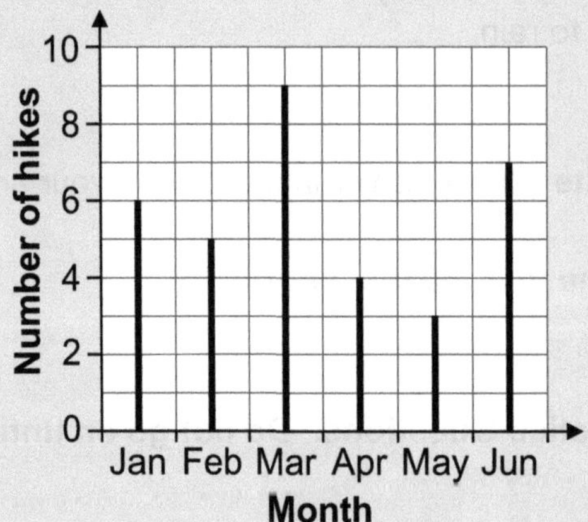

How many hikes did they go on in February and March in total?

A 5 **B** 14 **C** 9 **D** 11 **E** 15

P8 There are 84 chairs in an assembly hall.
The chairs are arranged in 12 equal rows.

How many chairs are in each row?

A 8   **B** 9   **C** 7   **D** 5   **E** 6

For the next two questions, write your answers in the boxes provided on your answer sheet (labelled P9 and P10). Any units needed are given on the answer sheet.

P9 **How many vertices does a triangular prism have?**

P10 There are 36 children in a school band. ¼ play brass instruments.

How many of the children do NOT play brass instruments?

End of Maths Practice Questions. Do not go on until you are told to.

English — Main Test

The sentences below contain either **one** punctuation mistake or **no** punctuation mistake. For each line, work out which group of words in the sentence contains a mistake and mark the letter on your answer sheet. **Mark N if there is no mistake.**

Punctuation Exercise

1 When she has time, my friend (Suzy enjoys dancing and playing table tennis.
   A   B   C   D   N

2 At 2 o'clock, Aoife, Lucy and rose are planning to take the train to Bangor.
   A   B   C   D   N

3 I'm sure Finn hasnt forgotten to feed the goldfish while you've been away.
   A   B   C   D   N

4 In Harper's house, you will certainly find paintings, cat's and plenty of plants.
   A   B   C   D   N

5 You'll need to bring three things tomorrow: some food, a jacket and a blanket.
   A   B   C   D   N

Choose the **best** word to complete each sentence below.
The sentences need to make sense and be written in correct English.
Pick **one** of the five options and mark the letter on your answer sheet.

Grammar Exercise

6   The view from the top of the hill is beautiful   **because   despite   and   since   after**   how
                                           A   **B**   **C**   **D**   **E**

    tiring it is to get there.

7   I thought that Georgina sang the song   **good   well   bad   great   perfect**   at the school
                                              A   **B**   **C**   **D**   **E**

    talent show last night.

8   Rabia and Harrison travelled   **in   around   by   with   at**   car to get to the water park.
                                   A **B** **C** **D** **E**

9   If Elizabeth wins this match,   **she'll   she's   she   her   hers**   make it through to the finals of
                                 A   **B**   **C**   **D**   **E**

    the tennis competition.

10   The purple trousers and yellow top,   **those   whose   that   whom   which**   no longer fit me,
                                   A   **B**   **C**   **D**   **E**

    are going to the charity shop.

Turn over to the next page

The sentences below contain some spelling mistakes. Each line has either **one** mistake or **no** mistake. For each line, work out which group of words contains a mistake and mark the letter on your answer sheet. **Mark N if there is no mistake.**

Spelling Exercise

11 William cooked a lovely breakfast for Jake because it was a specal occasion.

| A | B | C | D | N |

12 Isabelle said that her acommodation overseas was absolutely spotless.

| A | B | C | D | N |

13 After the difficult basketball match, sweat was leaking out of my pours.

| A | B | C | D | N |

14 Hassan will definitely win the baking competition with his chocolate cake.

| A | B | C | D | N |

15 Recently, Coralie has been experiencing a lot of tention in her lower back.

| A | B | C | D | N |

Read the **whole** passage carefully, then answer the questions that follow.

Cuneiform: A Mesopotamian Marvel

<u>**Contents**</u>

How Cuneiform Developed.. **line 6**

The Epic of Gilgamesh..**line 24**

Cracking the Cuneiform Code.......................................**line 37**

Thousands of years ago, in what is now Iraq, a brand new way of recording information
appeared — a type of writing called 'cuneiform'. Instead of drawing pictures of things, they started
making shapes in clay (called 'signs'), similar to how we use the letters of the alphabet today.
No-one today writes in cuneiform, but this ancient writing is still an incredible glimpse into the
5   distant past.

How Cuneiform Developed

In Ancient Mesopotamia, recording what you owned, bought or sold was done on pieces
of clay. The earliest clay tablets had pictographic* representations of animals and plants. As
communities grew larger, it became important to keep track of more detailed information — for
10   example, people needed to know exactly how much grain had been stored so they could be sure
there was enough to feed everyone. So, over time, people shifted away from drawing pictures
of things and started using signs to represent syllables — the units of sound that create words.
Using signs rather than drawing pictures meant that ancient people could now write about things
that they couldn't draw easily. This transition eventually led to cuneiform, the world's oldest
15   recorded writing system.

In order to make signs on the tablets (which were usually square or rectangular) the ancient
Mesopotamians shaped the clay while it was moist and malleable. A scribe* would press a stylus
into the clay to create indentations. The shape of the stylus, which was a stick usually cut from
a reed, affected how the writing looked: the name 'cuneiform' actually means 'wedge-shaped',
20   and refers to the distinctive shape of the indentations. Once a scribe had written everything they
needed to, they could leave the tablet to dry out in the sun. This would preserve the writing,
although if any of the text needed to be altered, simply dampening the clay would allow a scribe to
make any changes they wanted.

The Epic of Gilgamesh

25   While cuneiform was invented for trade and accounting, it proved useful for writing all kinds
of things. For example, one of the oldest works of literature was written in cuneiform: the 'Epic
of Gilgamesh'. The Epic of Gilgamesh is an epic poem that survives written on a number of
clay tablets, but there are still parts of the story that are missing as sadly many of the tablets
are damaged. However, the parts of the poem that are still readable continue to entertain and
30   captivate readers today.

*pictographic — *when a picture of something represents an idea or object*
*scribe — *someone whose job is to write out documents*

Turn over to the next page

The poem tells the story of a king named Gilgamesh, who wins a battle of strength against a ferocious man called Enkidu. After their contest, Gilgamesh and Enkidu become friends and the two characters travel together, but in the course of their adventures, Enkidu dies. Gilgamesh is so upset by Enkidu's death that he attempts to find the secret to eternal life, but despite all his efforts,
35 he fails. Although the Epic of Gilgamesh is a very old poem, readers still enjoy the themes of friendship, life and death, which feel relevant to them many centuries after the poem was written.

Cracking the Cuneiform Code

When people from later centuries saw cuneiform inscriptions on Mesopotamian buildings, they couldn't read the writing. It wasn't until the 18th century AD that historians tried to understand
40 cuneiform. In the years that followed, many scholars would attempt to crack the cuneiform code. Eventually, in the 1800s, researchers like Henry Rawlinson and Edward Hincks managed to decipher the writing system. For the first time in thousands of years, people could read cuneiform again.

The task of preserving cuneiform writing has now fallen to curators in museums. It takes years
45 of study to become an expert in cuneiform, so there aren't many people with the skills necessary to understand these incredible artefacts. This means there are many ancient tablets stored in museums that have still not been studied, and there is much that is yet to be learnt about the fascinating world of ancient Mesopotamia.

Answer these questions about the text. You can refer back to the text if you need to.
Pick the **best** answer and mark its letter on your answer sheet.

16 According to the text, why did the ancient Mesopotamians create a writing system?
    A So they could communicate with their friends.
    B So their businesses could make more money.
    C So they could relax and read stories.
    D So they could keep better records of information.
    E So they did not need to draw pictures any more.

17 What needs to be done in order to write cuneiform on a clay tablet?
Choose TWO.
    1. Pressing the stylus into the clay.
    2. Drying the reeds in the sun.
    3. Measuring the tablet to check it is square.
    4. Wetting the clay.
    5. Smoothing over any errors in the writing.

    A 1 and 3
    B 2 and 3
    C 1 and 4
    D 2 and 5
    E 4 and 5

18 **How could you find the part of the text that is about the development of cuneiform?**

  A   By checking the contents.
  B   By looking up the information online.
  C   By using a glossary.
  D   By checking the paragraph breaks.
  E   By reading the title of the text.

19 **Where does the name 'cuneiform' come from?**

  A   The process of drying the tablets in the sun.
  B   The softness of the clay that the scribes used.
  C   The rectangular shape of the clay tablets.
  D   The shape that the stylus made in the clay tablets.
  E   The material that was used to make a stylus.

20 **According to the text, why do readers continue to enjoy the Epic of Gilgamesh?**

  A   They are entertained by the missing parts of the poem.
  B   They like reading epic poetry more than accounting records.
  C   They think that Gilgamesh's adventures were epic.
  D   They find the topics covered in the poem relatable.
  E   They want to read something that was written thousands of years ago.

21 **In which century did researchers work out how to read cuneiform?**

  A   In the 21st century AD.
  B   In the 20th century AD.
  C   In the 19th century AD.
  D   In the 18th century AD.
  E   In the 17th century AD.

22 **Why hasn't every cuneiform tablet been translated?**

  A   It takes a long time to learn to read cuneiform.
  B   It is too time-consuming to preserve all of the tablets.
  C   There are not many tablets stored in museums.
  D   The curators don't want people to study them.
  E   It is exciting to keep some of the tablets mysterious.

Turn over to the next page

For these questions you have to **write your answers** neatly in the boxes provided on your answer sheet.

23 According to the text, who now has the role of preserving cuneiform writing?

24 According to the text, what would be used to make a stylus?

25 Which one word in lines 16-18 is closest in meaning to 'soft'?

26 Which six words in lines 28-30 explain why the Epic of Gilgamesh is not a complete poem?

27 Look at the sentence "After their contest..." (lines 32-33). Write all the verbs in this sentence.

28 Which ONE part of speech are the following words from the text?
distant (line 5), distinctive (line 20), ferocious (line 32), eternal (line 34)

Maths — Main Test

29 **Which of the following measurements is closest to 1.5 m?**

    A 1.25 m   **B** 1.7 m   **C** 166 cm   **D** 1490 cm   **E** 1.6 m

---

30 At a beach, there are 43 people in the water.
There are also 114 people on the sand.

How many people are at the beach altogether?

    A 130   **B** 157   **C** 147   **D** 121   **E** 150

---

31 Look at this shape.

How many lines of symmetry does the shape have?

    A 1   **B** 2   **C** 4   **D** 6   **E** 8

---

32 People in an online book club are asked what their favourite type of book is.
The pie chart shows the results.

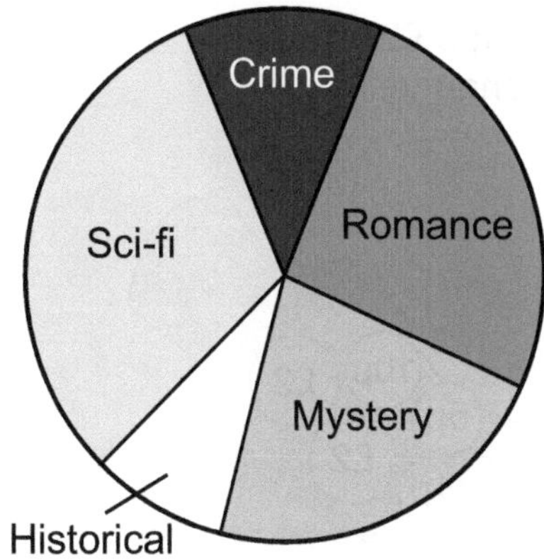

Which type of book is the most popular?

    A Sci-fi   **B** Crime   **C** Romance   **D** Mystery   **E** Historical

Turn over to the next page

33 A pot contains 0.55 kg of cooked rice.
One portion of cooked rice is 50 g.

How many portions of cooked rice can you make from the pot?

A   9 portions
B   7 portions
C   11 portions
D   5 portions
E   12 portions

---

34 Shabana has written a rule for a number sequence:

> Double the previous number, then subtract 5.

The sequence starts: 12, 19, 33...

What will the fifth number in the sequence be?

A   122   B   77   C   61   D   117   E   127

---

35 $a + 8 = 30$

What is the value of a?

A   38   B   28   C   22   D   12   E   32

---

36 Eoin pays for some groceries using a £20 note.
The shopkeeper hands Eoin his change.

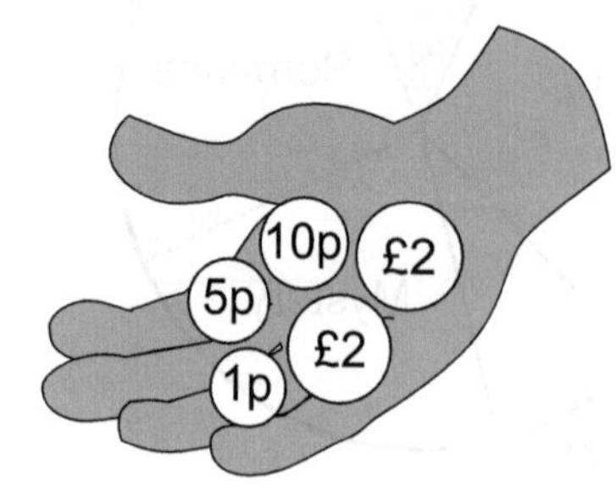

How much did Eoin's groceries cost?

A   £16.84   B   £15.84   C   £19.80   D   £16.16   E   £15.16

37 The rectangle below has been split into equal sections.

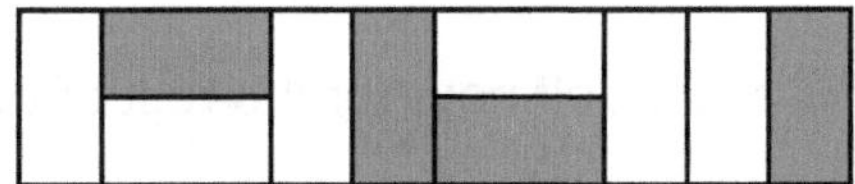

Some of the sections are shaded.

What proportion of the rectangle is shaded?

A 0.8   **B** 0.25   **C** 0.6   **D** 0.4   **E** 0.5

---

38 Mrs Bush measures the perimeter of her garden so she can build a fence around it.

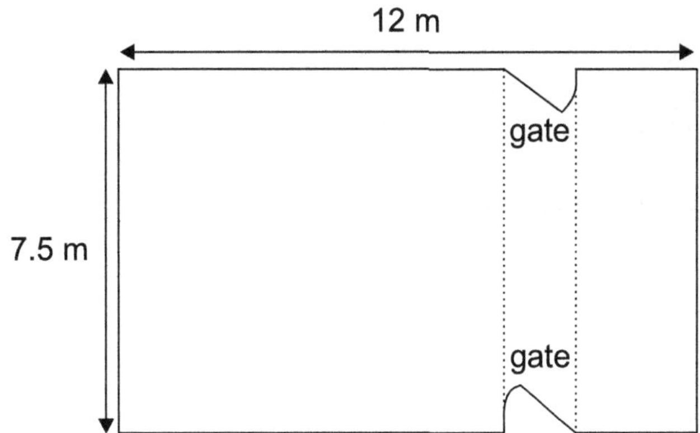

She needs to leave gaps for two gates. The gates are both 1.5 m wide.

What length of fence does Mrs Bush need for her garden?

A 39 m   **B** 37.5 m   **C** 36 m   **D** 34 m   **E** 36.5 m

---

39

Craft Shop	
Box of paper	£19.99
Pair of scissors	£7.48
Box of crayons	£8.75
Roll of tape	£1.55

Theo buys 1 box of paper, 3 rolls of tape and a pair of scissors.

Which of these is the best estimate for the total cost of Theo's items?

A £27   **B** £20   **C** £26   **D** £32   **E** £40

Turn over to the next page

40 Nora used a thermometer to measure the temperature at 5 pm.
The thermometer on the right shows Nora's reading.

The temperature fell by 1 °C every half hour for the rest of the day.

What was the temperature at 8:30 pm?

A   23 °C
B   20 °C
C   21 °C
D   18 °C
E   19 °C

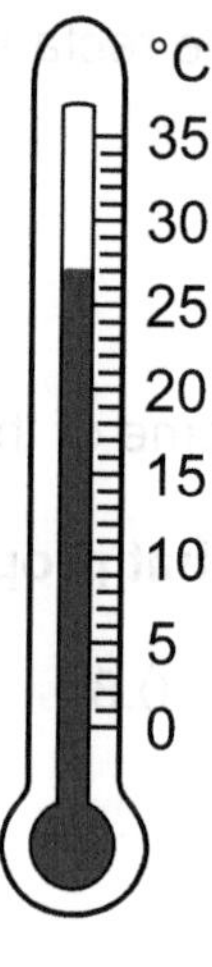

---

41 Yasmina and Leyla go to the cinema together.
Yasmina buys a large slushie (453 ml).
Leyla buys a green tea (226 ml) and a juice (215 ml).

Who buys more drink, and by how much?

A   Yasmina, by 2 ml
B   Leyla, by 8 ml
C   Yasmina, by 12 ml
D   Leyla, by 12 ml
E   Yasmina, by 4 ml

---

42 There are 8 different games at a school fair. Ahmed has already played 3 of them.
He randomly chooses one of the 8 games to play next.

What is the probability that Ahmed has NOT already played the game he chooses?

A $\frac{3}{8}$ B $\frac{3}{5}$ C $\frac{1}{8}$ D $\frac{5}{8}$ E $\frac{1}{5}$

---

43 6 people take part in a beach clean.
The table shows the number of pieces of rubbish collected by each person.

	Georgia	Nick	Tina	Kolo	Lupita	Seydou
Number of pieces collected	42	54	63	77	97	91

What is the range of the number of pieces of rubbish collected?

A   55   B   49   C   50   D   43   E   35

44 Tracey has an alarm set for 8:55 am on Saturday.

When she hits the 'snooze' button, 10 minutes pass before the alarm goes off again.
One Saturday, Tracey snoozes the alarm **4 times**.

When the alarm goes off for the fifth time, she switches it off and
stays in bed for another 12 minutes before getting out of bed.

What time does Tracey get out of bed?

A 9:57 am   **B** 9:35 am   **C** 10:02 am   **D** 9:47 am   **E** 9:23 am

---

45 The diagram shows the dimensions
of a cardboard box.

What is the volume of the cardboard box?

A 160 cm³
B 3200 cm³
C 1600 cm³
D 400 cm³
E 520 cm³

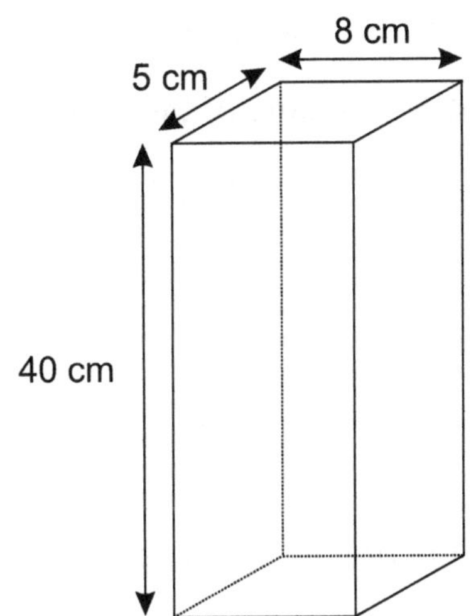

---

46 Kofi asked 30 of his classmates what their favourite type of music is.
He started making this tally chart of his results.

Type of Music	Tally
Pop	卌 |
Classical	|||
Rock	卌
Other	||

30% of his classmates chose pop.

How many more tally marks does Kofi need to add to the pop row?

A 3   **B** 9   **C** 6   **D** 2   **E** 10

Turn over to the next page

47 The points (3, 3) and (7, 3) are drawn on a coordinate grid.
A third point is drawn, and all three points are joined
to form an isosceles triangle.

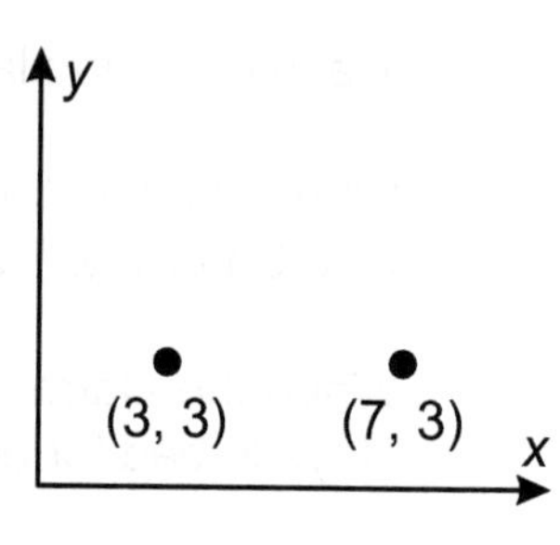

Which of these are possible coordinates of the third point?

A (5, 3)   **B** (3, 5)   **C** (3, 8)   **D** (5, 5)   **E** (7, 5)

---

48 A football match kicks off at 19:45 and lasts for 90 minutes.
Brendan arrives late at the stadium, at 19:54.

What percentage of the match does Brendan miss?

A 90%   **B** 9%   **C** 5%   **D** 20%   **E** 10%

---

49 Luke buys 4 ping pong balls and 1 paddle for £5.
Irfan buys 2 paddles from the same shop for £6.

What is the price of one ping pong ball?

A 75p   **B** £1   **C** 50p   **D** £0.25   **E** 10p

---

50 Five dogs took part in a competition.
They were scored out of 5 for Talent, Agility and Good Behaviour.

Dog	Talent	Agility	Good Behaviour
Woofer	4	2	2
Spot	3	3	5
Othello	5	2	3
Joker	4	4	1
Angel	2	5	5

All the talent scores were **doubled**, and the scores for each dog were added up.
The dog with the most points in total won.

Which dog won the competition?

A Woofer   **B** Spot   **C** Othello   **D** Joker   **E** Angel

For the following questions, write your answers in the boxes provided on your answer sheet.
Any units needed are given on the answer sheet.

51 Oliver has a packet of 30 mints.
He eats $\frac{1}{5}$ of them himself, then shares the rest out equally between Rita and Ruaridh.

How many mints does Oliver give to Ruaridh?

52 A scalene triangle is shown below.
Angle A is 47° and angle B is 121°.

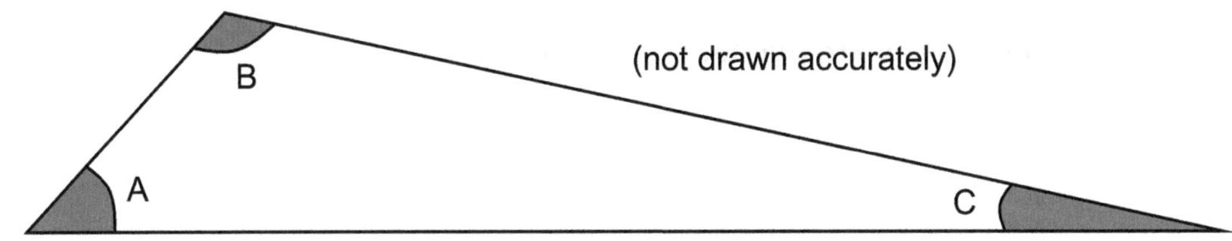

The angles in a triangle add up to 180°.

What is the size of angle C?

53 Below is part of a bus timetable for a village.

The Inn	12:22, 14:52, 16:47, 18:02
Village Hall	12:25, 14:55, 16:50, 18:05
High Street	12:28, 14:58, 16:53, 18:08
The Hill	12:30, 15:00, 16:55, 18:10

Russell leaves work at 16:30 and catches the next bus from The Inn.
He gets off at The Hill, then walks 3 minutes home.

How many minutes after leaving work does Russell arrive home?

Turn over to the next page

54 The table shows the number of fruit trees planted in an orchard.

Fruit	Number of Trees
Apple	30
Pear	
Plum	18
Cherry	28

TOTAL: 120

How many pear trees are planted in the orchard?

55

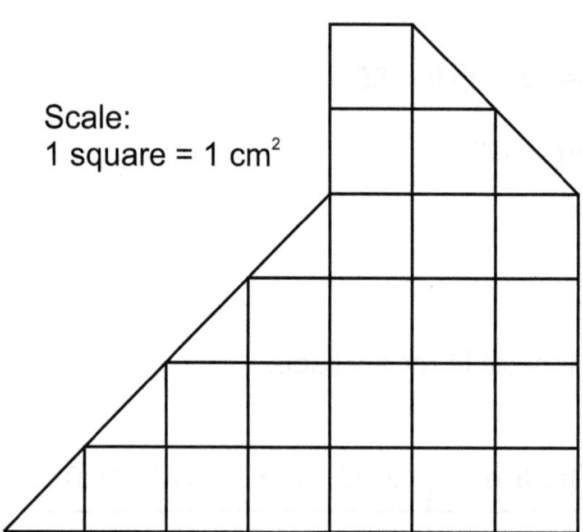

What is the area of the shape in cm²?

---

56 A newborn foal is 10 hands tall.
The foal grows into a horse which is 16 hands tall.
1 hand is equivalent to 10.2 cm.

How many centimetres taller is the horse than the newborn foal?

End of test

SEAG
Practice Paper

Set A: Paper 2

For the Entrance Assessment / Transfer Test

Read the following:

Do not start the test until you are told to do so.

1. At the start of this paper, there is a Practice Test, which has 5 English questions and 5 Maths questions. These questions will not be marked and are not timed.

2. The Main Test has 2 sections, English and Maths. There are 28 questions in each section. You have one hour to answer all the questions.

3. You should mark your answer to each question in pencil on the separate answer sheet. If you make a mistake, rub it out and mark your new answer clearly.

4. You should do any working out on a separate piece of paper.

English — Practice Test

The sentence below contains either **one** punctuation mistake or **no** punctuation mistake.
Work out which group of words in the sentence contains a mistake and mark the letter on
your answer sheet. **Mark N if there is no mistake.**

P1   Once you've walked for an hour or two, you'll see some house's in the distance.

      A   B   C   D   N

Choose the **best** word to complete the sentence. The sentence needs to make sense and be
written in correct English. Pick **one** of the five options and mark the letter on your answer sheet.

P2   Ella promised that she hadn't broken the toy **by of on at about** purpose.

      A B C D E

The sentence below contains either **one** spelling mistake or **no** spelling mistake.
Work out which group of words in the sentence contains a mistake and mark the
letter on your answer sheet. **Mark N if there is no mistake.**

P3   Unfortunatly he was unable to complete the race as he was exhausted.

      A   B   C   D   N

The Eiffel Tower

The Eiffel Tower is one of the most recognisable monuments in the world. First built to be one of the main attractions at the Paris World's Fair in 1889, the vast structure measures around 300 metres in height. At the time it was built, it was the world's tallest building, though it has since been overtaken by others, such as the Burj Khalifa.

5   The Eiffel Tower continues to be an immensely popular tourist attraction to this day, welcoming around seven million visitors every year. As well as being a stunning piece of architecture, the tower has also been home to several fascinating rooms throughout its history, including a post office, a theatre, an apartment for its creator (Gustave Eiffel) and a scientific laboratory.

For this question, choose **one** answer from the options below
and mark its letter on your answer sheet.

P4 According to the text, which of these statements about the Eiffel Tower is true?

- **A** It has fewer than five million visitors a year.
- **B** It was once home to an office building.
- **C** It is around 500 metres tall.
- **D** It is the world's tallest building.
- **E** It was an exhibit at the World's Fair.

For this question, you have to **write your answer** in the box on your answer sheet (box P5).

P5 Which one word from this text means 'interesting'?

End of English Practice Questions. Do not go on until you are told to.

Maths — Practice Test

Now try practice questions P6 to P10.
Read each question carefully before attempting to answer it.

P6 Zahra buys one item from a gift shop and pays with a £10 note.
She receives £2.10 in change.

Item	Price
Mug	£6.70
Cap	£7.90
Scarf	£8.10
Poster	£6.99
T-shirt	£8.90

Which item does she buy?

A Mug   **B** Cap   **C** Scarf   **D** Poster   **E** T-shirt

---

P7 The pictogram shows the number of different types of tree in a park.

Type of tree	Number of trees
Hazel	
Birch	
Oak	
Sycamore	

Key: = 4 trees

How many more birch trees are there than sycamore trees?

A 12   **B** 5   **C** 6   **D** 8   **E** 10

P8 Which of these numbers does NOT round to 300
when rounded to the nearest 100?

A 287   B 345   C 249   D 256   E 329

For the next two questions, write your answers in the boxes provided on your answer sheet
(labelled P9 and P10). Any units needed are given on the answer sheet.

P9 Kyle is 105 cm tall. Charlie is 5 cm taller than Kyle.

How tall is Charlie in metres?

P10 There are 50 houses in a street.
35 of the houses are painted white.

What percentage of the houses are painted white?

End of Maths Practice Questions. Do not go on until you are told to.

English — Main Test

The sentences below contain either **one** punctuation mistake or **no** punctuation mistake.
For each line, work out which group of words in the sentence contains a mistake and mark the
letter on your answer sheet. **Mark N if there is no mistake.**

Punctuation Exercise

1   Gauri sighed, looking at the map miserably. I think we've taken a wrong turn," she said.
     A   B   C   D   N

2   I said I'd take two kinds of jam — strawberry and damson to Eabha's birthday picnic.
     A   B   C   D   N

3   Under the sofa, Salma found a spider, some coins and her dog's favourite squeaky ball.
     A   B   C   D   N

4   As he walked onto the huge stage; Reuben knew one thing: he didn't feel nervous at all.
     A   B   C   D   N

5   "Have you seen my ruler" Maisy asked her dad. "I need it for a test at school tomorrow."
     A   B   C   D   N

Choose the **best** word to complete each sentence below.
The sentences need to make sense and be written in correct English.
Pick **one** of the five options and mark the letter on your answer sheet.

Grammar Exercise

6   The decorators have made a terrible mess —   **they'll they've they'd their them**
                                                      A   B   C   D   E

dripped paint all over the carpet.

7   Elena **waits will stand stands is waiting stood** on the beach and watched the sun
             A   B   C   D   E

set over the waves.

8   With that diving equipment, we could swim much **deeper deepest far shallow bigger**
                                                        A   B   C   D   E

than we ever have before.

9   Tomek took a picture of a group of **bear moose otter porcupine wolf** drinking from a
                                           A   B   C   D   E

river when he visited a national park In Canada.

10   Have you brought **fewer much too many various enough** samosas for everyone to
                         A   B   C   D   E

have at least one?

Turn over to the next page

The sentences below contain some spelling mistakes. Each line has either **one** mistake or **no** mistake. For each line, work out which group of words contains a mistake and mark the letter on your answer sheet. **Mark N if there is no mistake.**

Spelling Exercise

11 The magician raised her assistent in the air when she performed the levitation trick.

A	B	C	D	N

12 The cherry blosom drifted beautifully down from the trees in a cascade of pink petals.

A	B	C	D	N

13 Omar was an expert on volcanoes: he was very knowledgeable about magma and larva.

A	B	C	D	N

14 Ciara felt it was inappropriate to whisper during the solemn ceremony at the cathedral.

A	B	C	D	N

15 The plan to demolish the mansions wasn't sensable so the council abandoned the idea.

A	B	C	D	N

Read the **whole** passage carefully, then answer the questions that follow.

A Giant Adventure

"Everyone has a secret," my friend Cara declared one lunchtime at school.

"I'm not sure that's true," I replied through mouthfuls of cheese-and-pickle sandwich. "I don't think I have any secrets." I paused. "Well, not from you, anyway," I added, thinking guiltily about the chocolates I'd sneakily eaten that had turned out to be for Mum's party. She still had no idea
5   what had happened to them.

"It is true," she insisted. "And what's more, I think I've found out what my grandpa's secret was." She took a bite of her apple in what I can only imagine she thought was a mysterious way.

I rolled my eyes. "Don't be so cryptic, Cara. It doesn't suit—"

"7 o'clock tonight. At the stile by the stream. Be there."

10   I was used to Cara interrupting me, but before I could reply, the bell rang noisily. I'd been listening so intently that the sudden noise was as surprising as a firework exploding. By the time I'd composed myself, Cara had already gone.

I don't know what possessed me to show up, but at quarter past seven that night I found myself arriving at the old, slightly rotten stile. Cara was waiting for me.

15   "You're late," she said.

"Not like you to worry about the time," I replied. My teeth chattered; I pulled my coat around my shoulders. "Cara," I said with exasperation, "why have you dragged me out here?"

"I told you earlier! My grandpa's secret." Her eyes widened in the moonlight as she finally told me why we were there. "Gogmagog. I found my grandpa's diary. It said that when he was
20   younger, he found Gogmagog living here. But he likes privacy, so grandpa never told anyone."

"The giant?" I was stunned. I hadn't been expecting that. Gogmagog the giant wasn't real. We all knew the stories, of course — but they were just fairy tales for children!

She nodded at me and gestured towards the narrow rocky path ahead.

"Fine," I said testily. "We'll go out for a little bit, but when we don't find anything, we're going
25   straight home."

Cara smiled and handed me a torch. Together, we set off into the night. The pale moonbeams had illuminated our surroundings by the stile, but as the path wound its way deeper into a thicket of trees we became more reliant on the yellow torchlight. Every noise was magnified by the darkness. Dry leaves crunched under our feet like old newspaper. I struggled to keep up as Cara
30   strode confidently through the trees. She didn't seem to mind the sharp branches reaching into our path, scratching at our cheeks and arms with twigs like talons.

Suddenly, Cara stopped.

"We're here," she said. "These are the rocks my grandpa wrote about."

Turn over to the next page

I looked at the small pile of stones heaped on top of one another.

35   "Now what?" I asked. I didn't even try to sound interested. We'd been trekking for an hour and we'd seen neither hide nor hair of the legendary creature.

"We build a fire." Cara began moving the stones to form a small circle. I noticed she'd brought water with her. *Safety first*, I thought. I gathered some fallen branches and before long, we had a small cosy fire started.

40   Once I had warmed up, my mood lightened. Even though we hadn't seen the giant, when I looked into the fire, I found I didn't mind. Cara and I were silent as we watched the bright tendrils of flame stretch upwards towards the distant stars overhead.

Cara's sudden intake of breath roused me from my daydream. I felt a huge, looming presence behind me, but I was frozen to the spot. The figure moved and sat between us.

45   It was Gogmagog. Twelve feet tall, just as he'd always been described, he was larger than any creature I'd ever seen. He leant near the fire. I was sure he was about to roar. Instead, he spoke with a rich baritone voice.

"Have you got any o' them marshmallows?" Cara and I shook our heads as we gazed at him in shock. "Shame," he said, "I likes a nice toasted marshmallow on a night like this."

50   Cara was right when she said everyone has a secret. We've never told anyone about our experience, and if anyone asked, we'd say giants don't exist. But on pleasant evenings, we meet up, walk into the forest and munch on marshmallows with our friend, Gogmagog.

Answer these questions about the text. You can refer back to the text if you need to.
Pick the **best** answer and mark its letter on your answer sheet.

16   **"the sudden noise was as surprising as a firework exploding" (line 11).
      What is the name of the literary device used in this phrase?**

    A Personification
    B Direct address
    C Dialogue
    D Verse
    E Simile

17   **"My teeth chattered; I pulled my coat around my shoulders." (lines 16-17)
      What does this suggest about how the narrator feels?**

    A The narrator feels like talking to Cara.
    B The narrator feels very cold.
    C The narrator feels unsure about Cara's motivations.
    D The narrator feels annoyed with Cara.
    E The narrator feels apologetic after being late.

18 **What is the effect of the description of the trees in lines 30 to 31?**

   A It makes the trees in the forest sound very tall.
   B It makes the forest sound hostile and unwelcoming.
   C It makes it sound like there are very few trees.
   D It makes Cara seem scared of the forest.
   E It makes the forest seem fun.

19 **"...we'd seen neither hide nor hair of the legendary creature." (line 36)**
This suggests that:

   A they still didn't know what the giant looked like.
   B they had decided that the giant definitely wasn't real.
   C they had become very lost in the forest.
   D they hadn't found any evidence that the giant existed.
   E they don't like how hairy the giant is.

20 **Look at lines 40-42.**
How does the narrator feel in this paragraph?

   A The narrator feels more positive about being in the forest.
   B The narrator is worried that the fire might be dangerous.
   C The narrator feels it is better to be quiet than loud in the forest.
   D The narrator feels relieved that they haven't seen the giant.
   E The narrator thinks the forest Is a good place for looking at stars.

21 **Why were Cara and the narrator shocked when the giant started to talk?**

   A They thought that he would have a high and squeaky voice.
   B They were surprised that the descriptions of him were accurate.
   C They were worried because he was bigger than them.
   D Neither of them thought that the giant would actually appear.
   E They thought that the giant was going to scare them.

22 **Why do you think Cara and the narrator never told anyone about meeting the giant?**

   A Cara's grandpa made them promise they wouldn't tell anybody.
   B The narrator and Cara think it's important for everyone to have secrets.
   C Since the giant is their friend, they respect his wish for his location to stay unknown.
   D The narrator and Cara upset the giant because they didn't have any marshmallows.
   E After their encounter, Cara and the narrator never want to see the giant again.

Turn over to the next page

For these questions you have to **write your answers** neatly in the boxes provided on your answer sheet.

23 Look at lines 9-15. How many minutes later than Cara's suggested meeting time did the narrator actually arrive?

24 In which of her grandpa's belongings did Cara find out about the giant?

25 Which one word in lines 24-28 means the same as 'lit up'?

26 Which one word in lines 40-44 means the same as 'awakened'?

27 Which ONE part of speech are the following as they appear in the text?
guiltily (line 3), finally (line 18), testily (line 24), overhead (line 42)

28 Which part of speech is 'looming' as it appears in the text? (line 43)

Maths — Main Test

29 The bar chart shows how many coffees a shop sold over the course of one week.

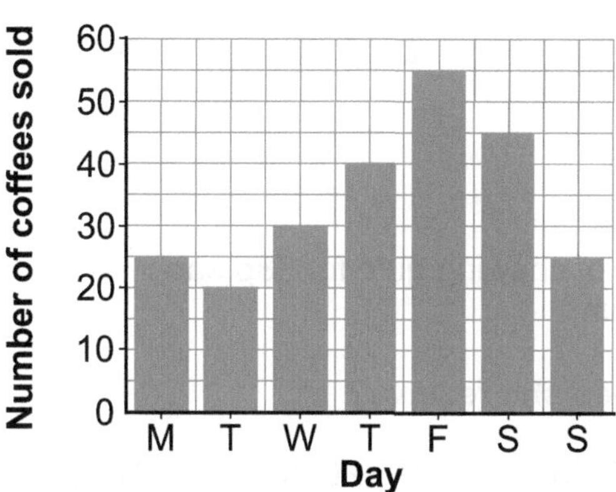

How many more coffees were sold on Friday than on Tuesday?

A 55   **B** 25   **C** 20   **D** 30   **E** 35

---

30 A pot contains 5 litres of soup.
Marissa's bowls hold 250 ml each.

How many bowls of soup can Marissa get from the pot?

A 10   **B** 20   **C** 16   **D** 25   **E** 100

---

31 Look at the numbers on this Venn diagram.

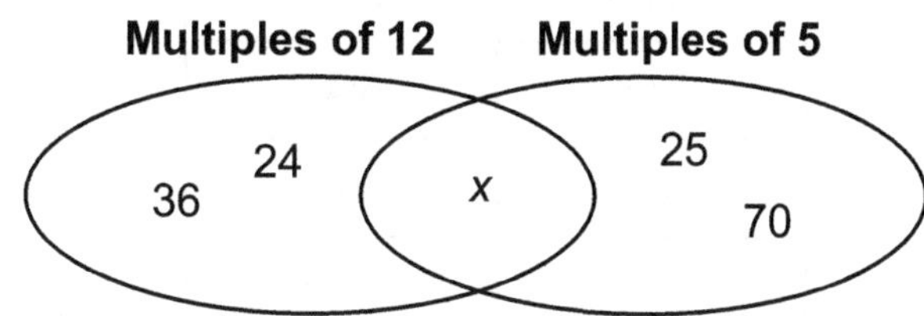

Which of these is a possible value for x?

A 30   **B** 48   **C** 60   **D** 65   **E** 72

Turn over to the next page

32 Usman is buying food for a barbecue.
He buys 9 packs of halloumi burgers and 7 packs of beef burgers.
There are 3 halloumi burgers per pack, and 4 beef burgers per pack.

**What is the difference between the number of beef burgers
and the number of halloumi burgers Usman buys?**

A 5   **B** 4   **C** 3   **D** 2   **E** 1

---

33 Corrina buys 3 packets of chewing gum for 68p each.
She pays with a £10 note.

How much change does she receive?

A £8.64   **B** £7.26   **C** £6.92   **D** £7.96   **E** £8.12

---

34 An arrow on a compass is pointing at North-East.

What type of turn does it need to make to point at South-East?

A One half turn clockwise
B Two quarter turns clockwise
C Three quarter turns clockwise
D One quarter turn clockwise
E One quarter turn anticlockwise

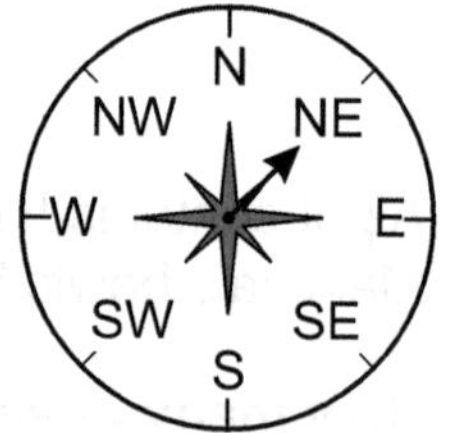

---

35 The table shows the time it took six competitors to finish a crossword.
The times are in minutes and seconds.

Name	Time
Amr	5:47
Bernie	5:42
Cho	6:01
Donal	5:50
Eleanor	5:34

Who finished third?

A Amr   **B** Bernie   **C** Cho   **D** Donal   **E** Eleanor

36 A function machine adds 7 to a number then divides the result by 3.
23 is put into the machine.

$$23 \longrightarrow \boxed{+\ 7} \longrightarrow \boxed{\div\ 3} \longrightarrow\ ?$$

What number comes out of the machine?

A 90   **B** 10   **C** 48   **D** 33   **E** 9

---

37 **Which set of coins is worth the smallest amount of money?**

A eighty-four 1p coins
B forty-three 2p coins
C three 20p coins and six 5p coins
D one 50p coin and two 20p coins
E four 10p coins and twenty 2p coins

---

38 An oil drum of height 1.62 m is raised up 1.53 m by a forklift truck.

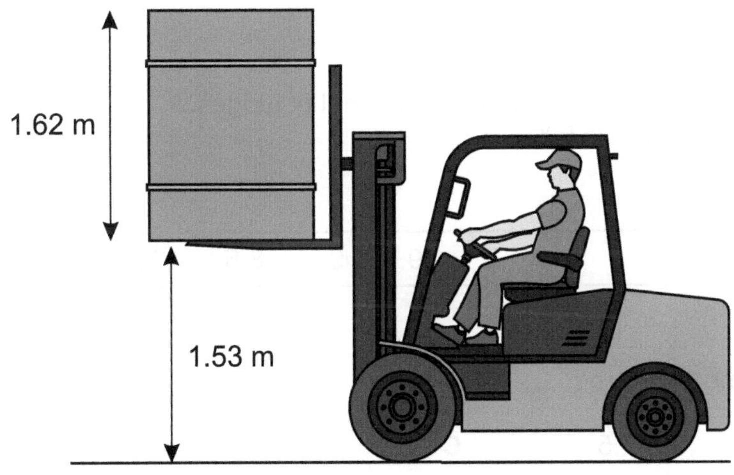

What is the distance from the ground to the top of the oil drum?

A 2.15 m   **B** 0.09 m   **C** 3.15 m   **D** 3.09 m   **E** 2.95 m

---

39 **What is 12 as a fraction of 36?**

A $\frac{3}{4}$ **B** $\frac{1}{12}$ **C** $\frac{1}{4}$ **D** $\frac{1}{3}$ **E** $\frac{1}{2}$

Turn over to the next page

40 This is an equilateral triangle. The angles in a triangle add up to 180°.

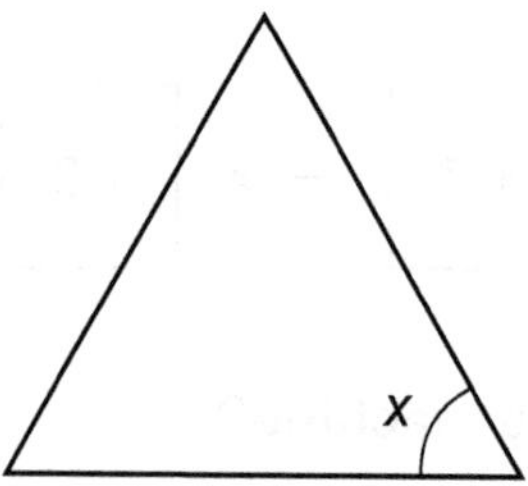

What is the size of angle _x_?

A 60°   **B** 90°   **C** 45°   **D** 30°   **E** 80°

---

41 This is the programme for a theatre show.

Which part of the show is the longest?

A Act I
B Act II
C Interval
D Act III
E Act IV

Theatre Programme

Act I   8:00   Act III 9:00
Act II   8:25   Act IV 9:20
Interval 8:45

SHOW ENDS AT **10:05**

---

42 Zola performs a gymnastics routine for a panel of judges.
The judges' scores are as follows:

7	8	7	9	9	8.5	7.5

What is her mean score?

A 7   **B** 7.5   **C** 8   **D** 8.5   **E** 9

---

43 **Which of these is NOT equivalent to 40%?**

A $\frac{8}{20}$ **B** $\frac{4}{10}$ **C** $\frac{2}{8}$ **D** $\frac{2}{5}$ **E** $\frac{20}{50}$

44 A tin of beans has a volume of 380 cm³.
The tin is a **quarter** full of beans.

What is the volume of beans in the tin?

A 100 cm³   **B** 85 cm³   **C** 190 cm³   **D** 90 cm³   **E** 95 cm³

---

45 Look at the following sequence.

| 1 | 3 | 6 | 10 | 15 | 21 | 28 | ..... |

What are the next two numbers in the sequence?

A 35, 43   **B** 36, 45   **C** 36, 44   **D** 35, 45   **E** 36, 46

---

46 The display shows the temperature of a walk-in freezer.

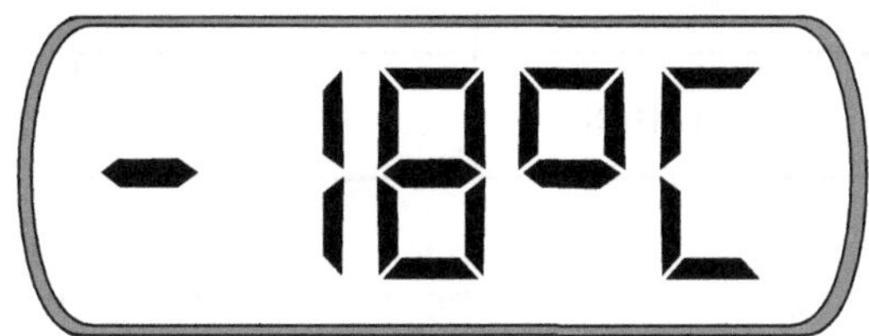

The door is left open overnight, and the temperature rises to 3 °C.

By how much did the temperature rise?

A 15 °C   **B** 11 °C   **C** 19 °C   **D** 21 °C   **E** 20 °C

---

47 **Which of the following values is prime?**

A 27 − 15
B 32
C 14
D 9 × 1
E 55 ÷ 5

Turn over to the next page

48 **Which of the following describes a square-based pyramid?**

A 6 faces, 8 vertices, 12 edges
B 5 faces, 5 vertices, 8 edges
C 5 faces, 6 vertices, 9 edges
D 5 faces, 5 vertices, 10 edges
E 4 faces, 4 vertices, 6 edges

---

49 A box of chocolates contains five different flavours.
The table shows the number of each flavour in the box.

Flavour	Number
Milk	11
White	4
Dark	3
Hazelnut	5
Caramel	7

Felipe reaches into the box and takes a chocolate at random.

What is the probability that it is a hazelnut chocolate?

A $\frac{1}{5}$ **B** $\frac{1}{3}$ **C** $\frac{1}{6}$ **D** $\frac{1}{10}$ **E** $\frac{5}{6}$

---

50 Penny goes to a pet store to buy some supplies.

<u>Pet Store</u>

Bag of treats	£6.50
Tin of cat food	£1.50
Litter tray	£9

She buys 1 bag of treats and 1 tin of cat food.
The store is having a sale, so Penny gets 25% off the total cost.

How much does Penny spend at the pet store?

A £8 **B** £6.75 **C** £6 **D** £2 **E** £7

For the following questions, write your answers in the boxes provided on your answer sheet.
Any units needed are given on the answer sheet.

51   This is part of a recipe for **five** cookies.

> Ingredients:
>
> 82 g of flour
> 60 g of butter
> 75 g of sugar

How many grams of flour are needed to make 20 cookies?

---

52   The chart shows the length of time in hours and minutes between some train stations.

Parkbury				
0:32	Barbham			
0:51	0:46	Anderton		
1:02	1:18	1:57	Dartley	
1:25	2:10	1:14	1:45	Otmel

Iggy takes the train from Otmel to Barbham.

How long does the journey take?

---

53   The width and length of a parking bay for a minibus is shown below.

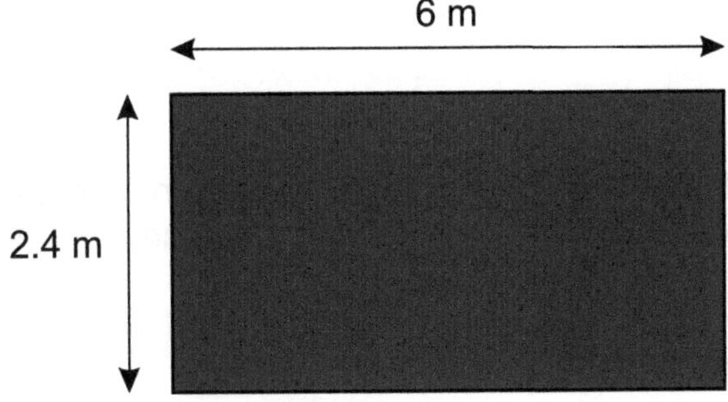

What is the area of the parking bay?

Turn over to the next page

54 The graph below shows the weight of a baby from birth to 6 months.

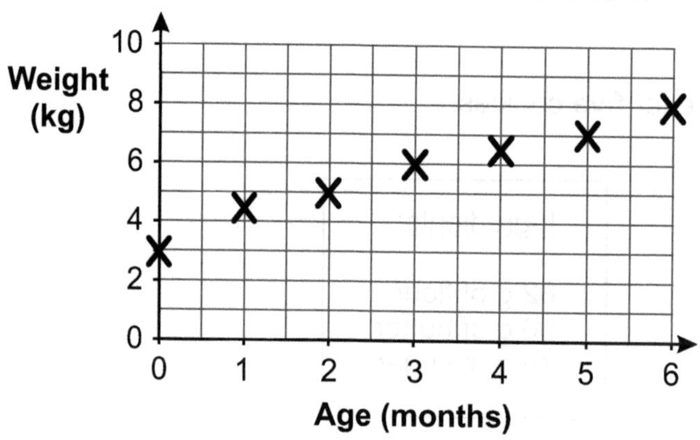

How much did the baby weigh at 5 months?

55 A shape is made from three regular pentagons joined together, as shown.

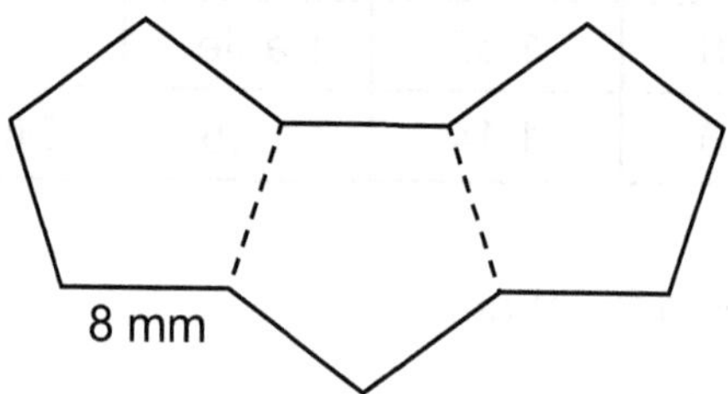

What is the perimeter of the shape?

56 Orla has baked 54 cupcakes for her office. There are seven other people in her office.
She shares all the cupcakes out equally (she doesn't take any for herself),
but some are left over.

How many cupcakes are left over?

End of test

SEAG
Practice Paper

Set B: Paper 1

For the Entrance Assessment / Transfer Test

Read the following:

Do not start the test until you are told to do so.

1. At the start of this paper, there is a Practice Test, which has 5 English questions and 5 Maths questions. These questions will not be marked and are not timed.

2. The Main Test has 2 sections, English and Maths. There are 28 questions in each section. You have one hour to answer all the questions.

3. You should mark your answer to each question in pencil on the separate answer sheet. If you make a mistake, rub it out and mark your new answer clearly.

4. You should do any working out on a separate piece of paper.

English — Practice Test

The sentence below contains either **one** punctuation mistake or **no** punctuation mistake.
Work out which group of words in the sentence contains a mistake and mark the letter on your answer sheet. **Mark N if there is no mistake.**

P1 Kalani has two hamsters: Jonathan has a gerbil, a guinea pig and a rabbit.

A	B	C	D	N

Choose the **best** word to complete the sentence. The sentence needs to make sense and be written in correct English. Pick **one** of the five options and mark the letter on your answer sheet.

P2 Eoghan likes cake **or** **before** **because** **unless** **so** it tastes delicious.

A	B	C	D	E

The sentence below contains either **one** spelling mistake or **no** spelling mistake.
Work out which group of words in the sentence contains a mistake and mark the letter on your answer sheet. **Mark N if there is no mistake.**

P3 Evelyn will probably be late to her apointment with the optician this afternoon.

A	B	C	D	N

Sita and the Snake

Sita had dreamed of owning a pet snake ever since she had seen a boa constrictor at her local zoo when she was a child. Now, her dream had come true. She had adopted a small, brown python from the animal shelter down the street and named her Sandy. She rushed home as fast as she could, excited to tell her flatmate the amazing news.

5   When she entered her apartment, she quickly set down Sandy's container on top of the living-room table before calling out to her flatmate.

"Tom, there's someone I'd like you to meet!" she yelled.

Tom appeared from the kitchen and dropped his bowl in shock when he heard a quiet hissing coming from the container.

10   In a timid whisper, he replied, "Please tell me that's not what I think it is..."

For this question, choose **one** answer from the options below
and mark its letter on your answer sheet.

P4   **Which of these things does Sita do after entering her apartment?**

    A Daydreams about owning a snake.
    B Visits a snake at the zoo.
    C Adopts a snake from the animal shelter.
    D Puts Sandy's container on the table.
    E Takes Sandy out of her container.

For this question, you have to **write your answer** in the box on your answer sheet (box P5).

P5   **Which one word from this text means 'nervous'?**

End of English Practice Questions. Do not go on until you are told to.

Maths — Practice Test

Now try practice questions P6 to P10.
Read each question carefully before attempting to answer it.

P6   Tariq has two 50p coins and three 10p coins. Matilda has one £2 coin.

How much more money does Matilda have than Tariq?

   A 30p   **B** 50p   **C** 80p   **D** 70p   **E** 60p

P7   Gráinne records the colours of the cars parked in the school car park.
She displays her results in this pie chart.

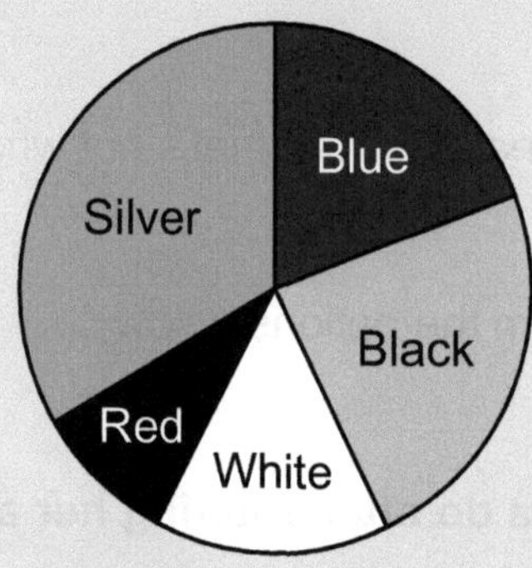

Which colour of car were there fewest of?

   A Blue   **B** Black   **C** White   **D** Red   **E** Silver

---

P8   A regular hexagon is shown below.

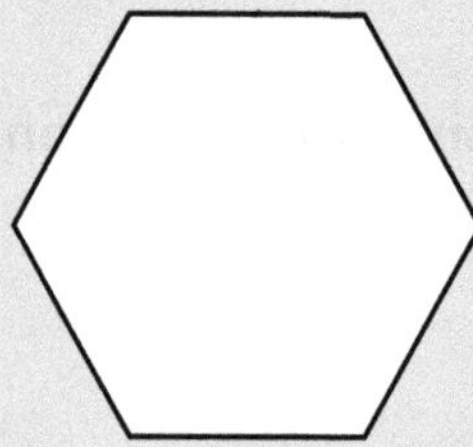

How many lines of symmetry does it have?

   A 1   **B** 2   **C** 3   **D** 4   **E** 6

For the next two questions, write your answers in the boxes provided on your answer sheet (labelled P9 and P10). Any units needed are given on the answer sheet.

P9 The table shows the heights that some children reached on a climbing wall.

Child	Height (m)
Cillian	4.7
Josie	5.5
Thibaut	3.9
Naresh	5.2
Shelly	4.1

How much higher did Josie climb than Thibaut?

P10 Three minibuses and two coaches arrive at a water park.
There are 20 people on each minibus and 60 people on each coach.

How many people are there on the minibuses and coaches in total?

End of Maths Practice Questions. Do not go on until you are told to.

English — Main Test

The sentences below contain either **one** punctuation mistake or **no** punctuation mistake.
For each line, work out which group of words in the sentence contains a mistake and mark the
letter on your answer sheet. **Mark N if there is no mistake.**

Punctuation Exercise

1 Timothy walked up to Rob and asked, "What are we having for breakfast?

        A   B   C   D   N

2 I'm thinking of buying a one-of-a-kind painting. Do you think that's a good idea?

        A   B   C   D   N

3 Danielle who (was very confused) waited impatiently for Declan's explanation.

        A   B   C   D   N

4 Abdul's daughter ate lots of vegetables today; broccoli, cauliflower and celery.

        A   B   C   D   N

5 I could'nt go to Theodore's costume party because my parrot (Lola) was ill.

        A   B   C   D   N

Choose the **best** word to complete each sentence below.
The sentences need to make sense and be written in correct English.
Pick **one** of the five options and mark the letter on your answer sheet.

Grammar Exercise

6   We should all go to the park this morning **despite   therefore   unless   whether   besides**
                                                    A   B   C   D   E

    you are too tired.

7   It is supposed to be very cold tomorrow so **I've   your   me   you'll   you're** have to bring
                                                  A   B   C   D   E

    a thick coat.

8   Róisín brought a selection of **cactus   cactus's   houseplant   cacti   houseplant's** to
                                       A   B   C   D   E

    grow on her windowsill.

9   Mohammed and his friends **were walking   are wandering   walking   walk   will wander**
                                     A   B   C   D   E

    to school when they spotted a beautiful bird.

10   Alexandra can run the **faster   fastest   quickly   strongest   well** out of everyone in her
                                A   B   C   D   E

    class at school.

Turn over to the next page

The sentences below contain some spelling mistakes. Each line has either **one** mistake or **no** mistake. For each line, work out which group of words contains a mistake and mark the letter on your answer sheet. **Mark N if there is no mistake.**

Spelling Exercise

11 Chandra sincerely apologysed to Benjamin for snatching the last slice of lemon cake.

| A | B | C | D | N |

12 If you're searching for a fabulous day out, I recomend going to the historic castle.

| A | B | C | D | N |

13 When I got the opportunity, I past the ball to Chris and he scored a dazzling goal.

| A | B | C | D | N |

14 The teacher began to doubt that Jessica had actually done her science homework.

| A | B | C | D | N |

15 I struggled to recognise her because she had changed her appearence dramatically.

| A | B | C | D | N |

Read the **whole** passage carefully, then answer the questions that follow.

The West Computers:
The Forgotten Stars of NASA

Neil Armstrong. Buzz Aldrin. Names familiar to anyone even vaguely interested in the history of space travel. However, despite what many think, the contributions of the men who travelled into space do not constitute the entire story. Forgotten about for years, marginalised during their lifetimes and overlooked in history are the large number of women, particularly African-American

5   women, who worked as mathematicians and engineers, and were integral to the achievements of NASA (the American 'National Aeronautics and Space Administration') in the 20th century and through to the present day.

In the early 1940s, facing the possibility of America's involvement in the Second World War, the NACA (NASA's predecessor) was confronted with the prospect of a huge loss of its workforce.

10   The National Advisory Committee for Aeronautics had already begun to hire white women with mathematics degrees as 'computers' — people who manually completed calculations that would later be done by electronic computers — but the threat of men being sent to war prompted an expansion of the team. In 1943, the Langley Memorial Aeronautical Laboratory, part of the NACA, began advertising for black women who were trained in mathematics. The female population

15   at Langley shot up, with an estimated 400 women working there by the mid-1940s. However, women were paid less than their male counterparts and were kept separate from the men. Black women were subject to even more discrimination: they were kept separate from the white women and were made to use segregated dining and bathroom facilities. They were dubbed 'The West Computers' because they worked at Langley's West Area whilst their white colleagues worked in

20   the East section. It was here that trailblazing women like Katherine Johnson, Dorothy Vaughan and Mary Jackson played their part in launching American astronauts towards the stars.

Johnson started work at Langley's West Area in 1953, crunching numbers for the NACA's engineers. After her arrival, she accidentally broke segregation rules by using a white women's bathroom. By the time she was aware of her mistake, she had no desire to change her routine

25   and no one told her otherwise — perhaps because her contributions to the NACA were so invaluable. These contributions included doing the calculations required for the USA's first human spaceflight in 1961 and helping to make John Glenn the first American to orbit the Earth. In 1969, her trajectory calculations helped to ensure that Apollo 11's monumental mission to the moon was successful.

30   Dorothy Vaughan also worked at Langley's West Area, and in 1949 she was appointed acting supervisor of the program, becoming the first African-American woman to receive a promotion at the NACA. She remained there for 28 years and was a master of FORTRAN, an early computer programming language. Another of the most notable West Computers was Mary Jackson, who became NASA's first black female engineer in 1958. After receiving the most senior engineering

35   title available in the 1970s, she turned her attention towards working to increase female representation at NASA as manager of both the Federal Women's Programme (responsible for enhancing employment opportunities for women) and the Affirmative Action Programme (responsible for increasing diversity and removing discrimination in the workplace).

Turn over to the next page

Though the West Computers' efforts were vital in helping the USA win the space race* and

40 achieve numerous scientific breakthroughs in the 20th and 21st centuries, their contributions were relatively unknown for years. Whilst the male faces of space missions became front-page news, strikingly missing from most stories were the women who made it all possible. However, in recent years, the tide has begun to turn. In 2015, President Obama awarded Katherine Johnson the Presidential Medal of Freedom for her incredible work. In 2016, Margot Lee Shetterly published

45 *Hidden Figures: The Untold Story of the African American Women Who Helped Win the Space Race*, detailing the lives and achievements of Johnson, Vaughan and Jackson, and later that year an adaptation of the book hit the screens as an award-winning film.

Katherine Johnson. Dorothy Vaughan. Mary Jackson. Women who, along with many others, overcame barriers of racial prejudice and gender discrimination, and changed space science

50 forever. Now they are finally receiving their well-earned spot among the stars of scientific history.

Bibliography

Katherine Johnson, "My Remarkable Journey: A Memoir"

Margot Lee Shetterly, "Hidden Figures: The Untold Story of the African American Women Who Helped Win the Space Race"

**space race — in the 20th century, the USA and the Soviet Union competed to be the best at advancing space exploration and technology.*

Answer these questions about the text. You can refer back to the text if you need to.
Pick the **best** answer and mark its letter on your answer sheet.

16 **"Names familiar to anyone even vaguely interested in the history of space travel" (lines 1-2). This means that:**

    A Only people who know lots about space travel will have heard of those names.
    B Only people with a slight interest in space travel will know those names.
    C Those names are only interesting to people who study the history of space travel.
    D Those names aren't related to the history of space travel.
    E You don't need to know very much about space travel to have heard of those names.

17 **According to the text, why did the NACA begin to recruit women?**

    A Because many of their staff had died in WWI.
    B Because segregation was coming to an end.
    C Because they wanted to improve diversity at the NACA.
    D Because they recognised how helpful women could be.
    E Because WWII would cause a shortage in their staff.

18 **According to the text, how were black women working at Langley treated differently? Choose TWO.**

1. Black women were paid more than white women.
2. White women mixed with men but black women were kept separate.
3. Black women had to eat in separate places to white women.
4. Black women weren't allowed to use electronic computers.
5. Black women were made to use different toilets.

   A 1 and 3
   B 2 and 5
   C 1 and 4
   D 3 and 5
   E 4 and 5

19 **Katherine Johnson's "contributions to the NACA were so invaluable." (lines 25-26) What does this tell you about Katherine's work?**

   A Her work could have been done by anyone.
   B Her work made lots of money for the NACA.
   C Her work was more important than anyone else's.
   D Her work involved using equipment that was very expensive.
   E Her work was very important to the NACA.

20 **Which of these was one of Katherine Johnson's achievements?**

   A She was manager of the Affirmative Action Programme.
   B She made the trajectory calculations for the 1969 moon landing.
   C She was NASA's first black female engineer.
   D She was the first African-American woman to receive a promotion at the NACA.
   E She was a master at FORTRAN.

21 **In which year was a film about the West Computers released?**

   A 2015
   B 2016
   C 2017
   D 2018
   E 2019

22 **According to the text, which of the following helped to publicise the work and achievements of the West Computers?**

   A The USA winning the space race.
   B Front-page newspaper articles.
   C The Federal Women's Programme.
   D Margot Lee Shetterly's book.
   E Katherine Johnson's memoir.

Turn over to the next page

For these questions you have to **write your answers** neatly in the boxes provided on your answer sheet.

23   **What does the acronym NACA stand for?**

24   **Which of the West Computers received the Presidential Medal of Freedom?**

25   **Which one word in lines 8-14 is closest in meaning to 'increase'?**

26   **Which six words in lines 41-44 explain that the perception of the West Computers has changed?**

27   **Look at the sentence "However, despite what many think..." (lines 2-3). Write all the verbs in this sentence.**

28   **Which ONE part of speech are the following words from the text? less (line 16), accidentally (line 23), most (line 33), relatively (line 41)**

Maths — Main Test

29 Some children took part in a swimming race. The table below shows their times.

Name	Time (seconds)
Rahul	59
Callum	56
Alyssa	42
Maeve	34
Cian	49

What is the range of the data?

A 10 s   **B** 30 s   **C** 25 s   **D** 17 s   **E** 3 s

---

30 **Which of the following statements is true for a rectangle?**

A It has four lines of symmetry.
B It doesn't have any right angles.
C All of its angles are different.
D It has two pairs of equal-length sides.
E All of its sides are the same length.

---

31 Mr O'Brein left home at 14:35 and drove to the shops. The drive took him 14 minutes.
He spent 28 minutes shopping. He then drove back home, which took him 16 minutes.

At what time did Mr O'Brein arrive back at home?

A 15:19   **B** 16:33   **C** 15:33   **D** 15:17   **E** 15:05

---

32 **Which of the following values is NOT equivalent to the others?**

A 30%   **B** $\frac{1}{3}$ **C** $\frac{3}{10}$ **D** 0.3   **E** $\frac{30}{100}$

Turn over to the next page

33 This Venn diagram shows some properties of 3D shapes.

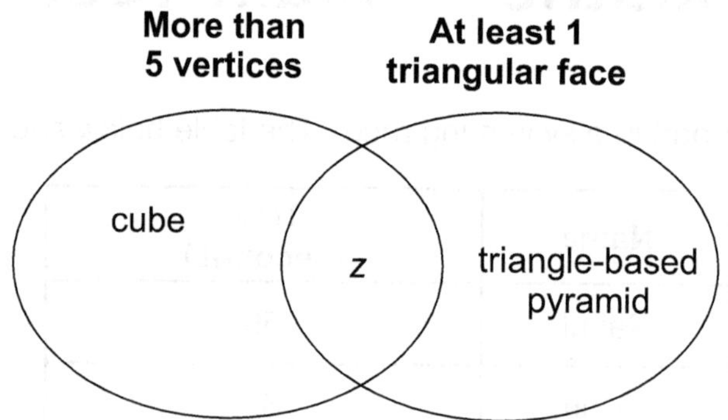

What shape could *z* be?

A Cylinder
B Cuboid
C Square-based pyramid
D Cone
E Triangular prism

---

34 It takes a machine 6 minutes to make 8 boxes.

How long does it take the machine to make 96 boxes?

A 128 minutes
B 1 hour and 12 minutes
C 1 hour and 36 minutes
D 112 minutes
E 54 minutes

---

35 A shop sells apples for 36p each and bananas for 21p each.
Devi buys 10 apples and 6 bananas. She pays with a £10 note.

How much change does Devi receive?

A £5.14   B £4.26   C £4.86   D £5.24   E £5.54

---

36 The table below shows the number of different coloured T-shirts in a shop.

Colour	Pink	Yellow	Blue	Green	White
Number	8	4	10	6	12

What fraction of the T-shirts are white?

A $\frac{4}{10}$ B $\frac{3}{10}$ C $\frac{1}{4}$ D $\frac{3}{20}$ E $\frac{1}{5}$

37 This bar chart shows the number of times some children have been to the cinema in the last year.

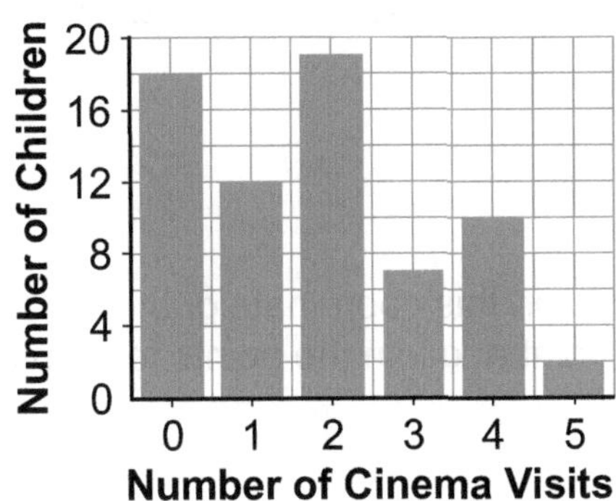

How many children have been to the cinema fewer than two times in the last year?

A 30 **B** 18 **C** 49 **D** 17 **E** 34

---

38 A sequence starts 2, 6, 18, 54...

What is the next number in the sequence?

A 216 **B** 162 **C** 92 **D** 108 **E** 90

---

39 Look at the map below. The distances between the three towns on the map have been measured with a ruler.

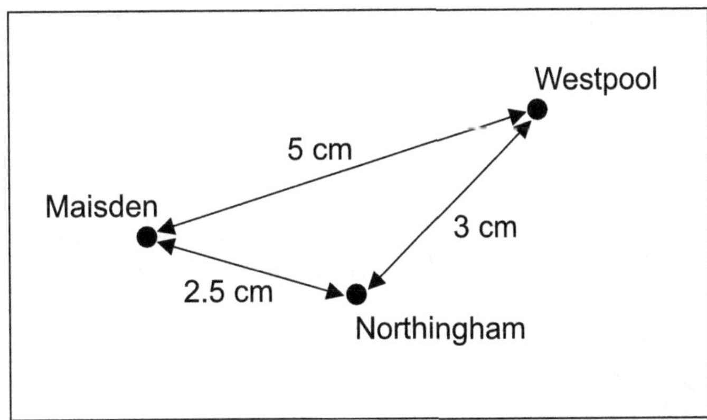

The scale for this map is 1 cm = 5 km.

How far apart are Maisden and Westpool in real life?

A 50 km **B** 12.5 km **C** 5 km **D** 15 km **E** 25 km

Turn over to the next page

40 **Which of the following is NOT a square number?**

A 100   **B** 36   **C** 49   **D** 56   **E** 121

---

41 David has marked three points on this coordinate grid.
He is going to mark a fourth point and join the points to form a parallelogram.

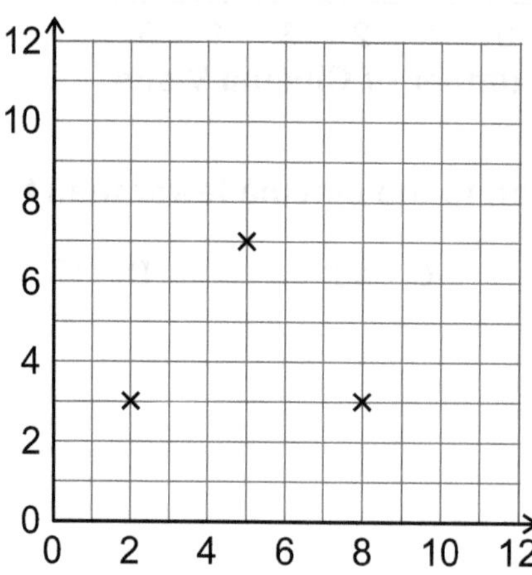

Which of these are the coordinates of the fourth point?

A (2, 11)   **B** (0, 7)   **C** (10, 7)   **D** (5, 0)   **E** (11, 7)

---

42 The mass of 3 bags of flour is 4.5 kg. The mass of 5 bags of sugar is 2500 g.

What is the difference in mass between one bag of flour and one bag of sugar?

A 1 kg   **B** 0.2 kg   **C** 1.5 kg   **D** 0.5 kg   **E** 2 kg

---

43 Liana arrived home from work in the afternoon and decided to have a nap.
The clocks show the times when she fell asleep and woke up.

Time Liana fell asleep

Time Liana woke up

In hours and minutes, how long did Liana nap for?

A 0:45   **B** 1:30   **C** 2:15   **D** 1:15   **E** 1:20

44 **What is 30.02 × 100?**

A 300.2   B 3200   C 3002   D 302   E 3020

45 There are 80 pens in a box. 12 of the pens are red and the rest are black.
Arlo chooses a pen at random from the box.

What is the probability that Arlo chooses a black pen?

A 65%   B 85%   C 50%   D 75%   E 90%

46 Nina is planning to sell some records. She uses a pictogram to group the records
into three categories: Mint Condition, Good Condition, and Used Condition.

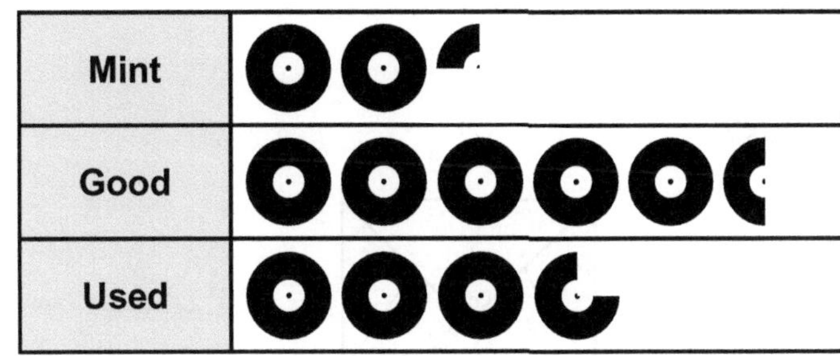

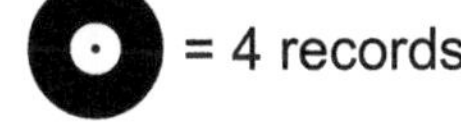

How many records is Nina selling in total?

A 46   B 23   C 40   D 32   E 43

47 **Which of these numbers has BOTH 7 and 8 as factors?**

A 42   B 64   C 84   D 56   E 72

Turn over to the next page

48 Twins Raj and Prisha had their heights measured.
Raj was 1.23 m tall and Prisha was 1.17 m tall.
Since then, Raj has grown by 7 cm and Prisha has grown by **twice as much as Raj**.

Who is taller now, and by how much?

A Prisha, by 1 cm
B Raj, by 3 cm
C Prisha, by 5 cm
D Raj, by 7 cm
E Prisha, by 14 cm

---

49 Zena receives £2.50 pocket money a week. She saves all her pocket money for 16 weeks.
She spends £11.50 on a bracelet.

How much money does Zena have left?

A £31.00   **B** £33.50   **C** £28.50   **D** £36.00   **E** £26.00

---

50 **How heavy is this box?**

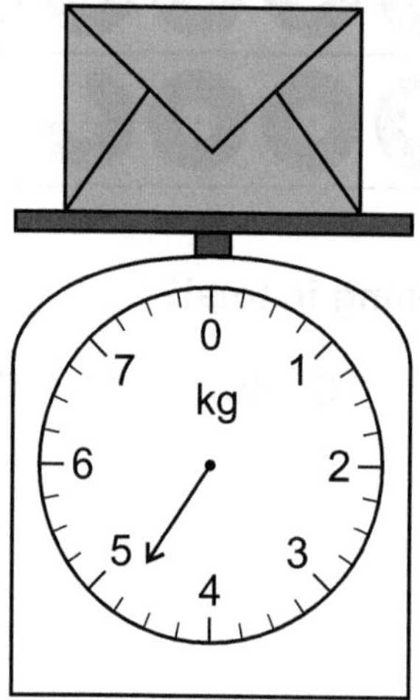

A 4.9 kg   **B** 4750 g   **C** 475 g   **D** 4.8 kg   **E** 4.5 kg

For the following questions, write your answers in the boxes provided on your answer sheet.
Any units needed are given on the answer sheet.

51 Look at these two overlapping rectangles.

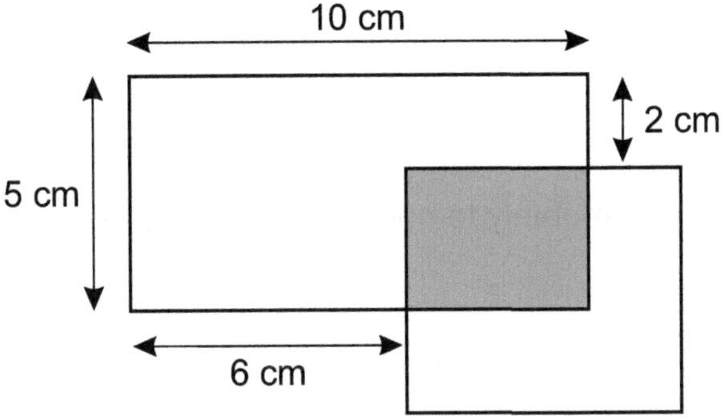

What is the area of the overlap, shaded in grey?

---

52 Fionn is making caramel. He needs to heat the sugar to 160 °C.
This thermometer shows the temperature of the sugar after he has heated it for 5 minutes.

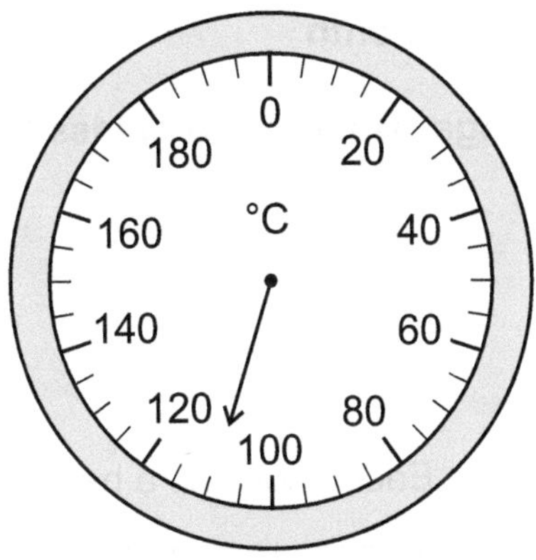

The sugar then increases in temperature by 10 °C every 30 seconds.

How long, in minutes and seconds, does Fionn heat the sugar for in total?

---

53 Bridget buys 1 museum ticket and 6 souvenir postcards for £24.
Shauna buys 3 museum tickets for £45.

How much does one souvenir postcard cost?

Turn over to the next page

54 Isla is making a plant pot and saucer out of clay.
She needs 400 g of clay to make the plant pot and 340 g of clay to make the saucer.
Isla has 3 blocks of clay, which have masses of 114 g, 97 g and 105 g.

How much more clay does Isla need to make the plant pot and saucer?

55 This graph shows the average monthly temperature for a city over one year.

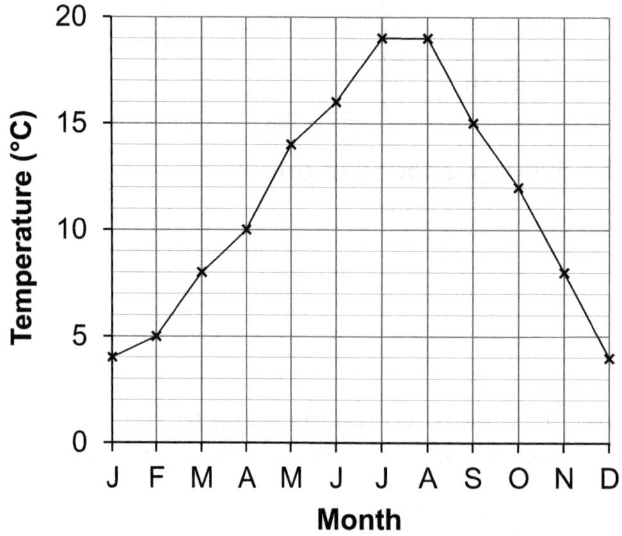

How many months have an average temperature of less than 11 °C?

56 Look at this bridge made from bricks. Each brick has a height of 30.5 cm.

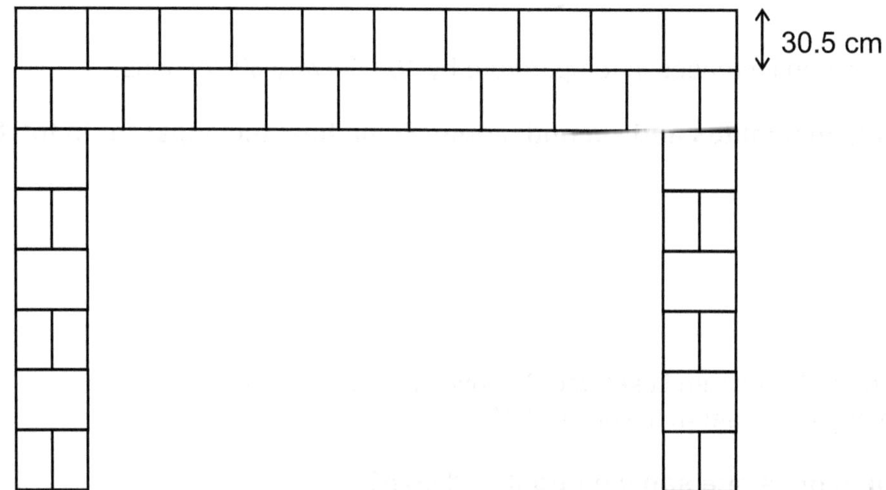

How tall is the bridge in centimetres?

End of test

SEAG Practice Paper

Set B: Paper 2

For the Entrance Assessment / Transfer Test

Read the following:

Do not start the test until you are told to do so.

1. At the start of this paper, there is a Practice Test, which has 5 English questions and 5 Maths questions. These questions will not be marked and are not timed.

2. The Main Test has 2 sections, English and Maths. There are 28 questions in each section. You have one hour to answer all the questions.

3. You should mark your answer to each question in pencil on the separate answer sheet. If you make a mistake, rub it out and mark your new answer clearly.

4. You should do any working out on a separate piece of paper.

English — Practice Test

The sentence below contains either **one** punctuation mistake or **no** punctuation mistake. Work out which group of words in the sentence contains a mistake and mark the letter on your answer sheet. **Mark N if there is no mistake.**

P1 Arabella, my sister's best friend, has long blonde hair and, is very tall.

    A   B   C   D   N

Choose the **best** word to complete the sentence. The sentence needs to make sense and be written in correct English. Pick **one** of the five options and mark the letter on your answer sheet.

P2 I was **the a this an that** only tour guide who worked on Fridays.

   A B C D E

The sentence below contains either **one** spelling mistake or **no** spelling mistake. Work out which group of words in the sentence contains a mistake and mark the letter on your answer sheet. **Mark N if there is no mistake.**

P3 Ali let out a loud shreik when he spotted the spider crawling on the ceiling.

    A   B   C   D   N

Caroline Haslett

Born in 1895, Caroline Haslett was an electrical engineer who spent her life striving to improve opportunities and conditions for women in the workplace. Following a stint as a clerk for a boiler firm, Haslett eventually trained in a more practical role. By 1919, she had qualified as an engineer and taken up a leading position in the newly formed Women's
5 Engineering Society.

One of Haslett's main endeavours was to promote electrical devices that would revolutionise household chores. Since the majority of such tasks fell to women, Haslett was keen to educate them about how electricity could make their lives easier. Throughout her career she fought for women to have the right to work in all kinds of jobs and be paid fair
10 wages. She is regarded as a pioneer for women in the worlds of engineering and business.

For this question, choose **one** answer from the options below
and mark its letter on your answer sheet.

P4 **Why did Caroline Haslett think electricity could be useful to women?**

    A Because it would help them focus on their chores.
    B Because the Women's Engineering Society thought so.
    C Because it would help them to get good jobs.
    D Because it would inspire them to become electrical engineers.
    E Because it would make domestic chores easier.

For this question, you have to **write your answer** in the box on your answer sheet (box P5).

P5 **Which one word from this text means 'transform'?**

End of English Practice Questions. Do not go on until you are told to.

Maths — Practice Test

Now try practice questions P6 to P10.
Read each question carefully before attempting to answer it.

P6   Look at the time shown on the clock.

What time will it be 15 minutes later?

A   3:30   **B**   2:45   **C**   3:45   **D**   2:15   **E**   2:30

P7   Zach has a 500 g bag of flour. He uses some flour to make a cake.
The scale shows how much flour is left in the bag.

How much flour did Zach use in his cake?

A   350 g   **B**   400 g   **C**   150 g   **D**   100 g   **E**   250 g

P8 Aisling has 20 animals on her farm. There are 8 cows and the rest are sheep.

What fraction of her animals are sheep?

A ½   **B** ⅗   **C** ⅖   **D** ⅔   **E** ¾

For the next two questions, write your answers in the boxes provided on your answer sheet (labelled P9 and P10). Any units needed are given on the answer sheet.

P9 This Venn diagram shows some information about Class 6's pet dogs.

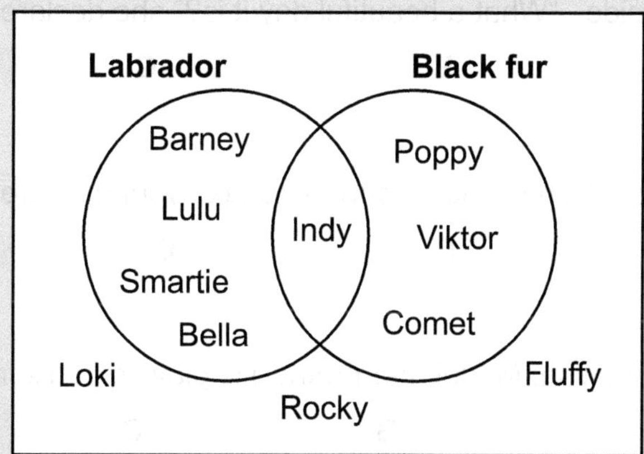

How many Labradors are there?

P10 There are 80 children in a year group. 25% of them play football.

How many children play football?

End of Maths Practice Questions. Do not go on until you are told to.

English — Main Test

The sentences below contain either **one** punctuation mistake or **no** punctuation mistake. For each line, work out which group of words in the sentence contains a mistake and mark the letter on your answer sheet. **Mark N if there is no mistake.**

Punctuation Exercise

1 When Jakub saw the food. he realised how much he'd missed his mother's cooking.

    A   B   C   D   N

2 Charlotte glanced outside. "What a beautiful day it is?" she declared with a smile.

    A   B   C   D   N

3 "Wherever you go," said Reggie, "its important to take your cat's treats with you."

    A   B   C   D   N

4 Maryam has gone swimming; Medhi (her brother) is playing in his friend's garden.

    A   B   C   D   N

5 After his morning jog, Joe immediately, went back home and had a well-deserved nap.

    A   B   C   D   N

Choose the **best** word to complete each sentence below.
The sentences need to make sense and be written in correct English.
Pick **one** of the five options and mark the letter on your answer sheet.

Grammar Exercise

6   When my family went hiking, we took a map **if** **despite** **unless** **until** **so** we wouldn't
                                                             A   B   C   D   E

get lost in the forest.

7   The actor **practised** **will rehearse** **is practising** **practise** **prepares** his big speech
               A   B   C   D   E

every day before he performed.

8   Gavin was the first one to notice that his sister was wearing **mine** **my** **she** **he** **him**
                                                               A B C D E

denim jacket.

9   Francesca's garden contains the **higher** **height** **taller** **tallest** **very high** tree
                                A   B   C   D   E

in the entire village.

10   Do you know the man **what** **which** **whose** **who's** **who** works with Rebecca?
                                      A   B   C   D   E

Turn over to the next page

The sentences below contain some spelling mistakes. Each line has either **one** mistake or **no** mistake. For each line, work out which group of words contains a mistake and mark the letter on your answer sheet. **Mark N if there is no mistake.**

Spelling Exercise

11 The chemist poured a bright green substence into the beaker and it started to bubble.

A	B	C	D	N

12 A nearby town had recently experienced a hurricane and was struggling to recover.

A	B	C	D	N

13 The teacher didn't think that Owen's story was particularly relevent to our lesson.

A	B	C	D	N

14 My dress is slightly too long currently — I will have to get someone to altar it for me.

A	B	C	D	N

15 Ibrahim thought that the novel was humorous but he found the protagonist insufferible.

A	B	C	D	N

Read the **whole** poem carefully, then answer the questions that follow.

The Last Garden

The trees were felled and not replaced,
The birds ceased singing in the skies,
The world became a vast, grey waste —
A bleak and miserable demise.

5   But in my patch of barren earth,
Where I thought nothing grew at all,
A shoot emerged, the very first
I'd seen since nature's sad downfall.

I felt my heart lift at the sight
10   Of one small pair of tiny leaves.
I knew I'd try with all my might
To help this scrawny plant succeed.

I built a screen to shield it from
The harsh winds threatening all around.
15   I brought some water; poured it on
The sun-baked, parched and dusty ground.

And slowly upwards grew the shoot,
Emerging more and more each day.
And ever deeper drove its roots
20   Which battled solid soil and clay.

And how it grew! For many weeks
I watched it tentatively climb
And stretch its multiplying leaves
Despite the blazing hot sunshine.

25   Its flowers bloomed, but faded soon,
Then out of it fell seven seeds.
So once more, I began anew
To tend the seedlings' growing needs.

Each spring more shoots rose from the dirt.
30   My trees grew tall as mountains are.
A paradise, circled by a desert,
With flowers numerous as stars.

And then the animals returned!
So many creatures now moved in,
35   Like beetles, spiders, snails and worms.
And insects with mosaic wings.

And people too — from far and wide
They travel here to visit
The only place not burnt and dried;
40   My garden lifts their spirits.

To every visitor that comes,
And views my verdant plot,
I gift some seeds and tools and gloves,
To make themselves a thriving spot.

45   I hope my lonely garden won't
Remain the only one that's here.
I hope you'll build a better home,
And that a greener future's near.

Answer these questions about the text. You can refer back to the text if you need to.
Pick the **best** answer and mark its letter on your answer sheet.

16   **Which of these statements about the poem's rhyme scheme is true?**

   A   The first and second lines of each stanza rhyme.
   B   The second and third lines of each stanza rhyme.
   C   The third and fourth lines of each stanza rhyme.
   D   The second and fourth lines of each stanza rhyme.
   E   None of the lines in any of the stanzas rhyme.

Turn over to the next page

17 How did seeing the first leaves of the plant make the speaker of the poem feel?

A Hopeful
B Tired
C Upset
D Astonished
E Generous

18 What is the effect of the exclamation mark in line 21?

A It shows the speaker is unenthusiastic about the plant.
B It shows the speaker's excitement about the plant's growth.
C It shows the speaker didn't know much about plants.
D It shows the speaker was impatient for the plant to grow.
E It shows the speaker dislikes the plant.

19 Look at lines 21-28.
Which of these statements describe what happens in the stanzas? Choose TWO.
1. The speaker counted all of the plant's leaves.
2. The speaker feels guilty that the plant died.
3. The speaker observed the plant's slow growth.
4. The speaker collected all of the new seeds to plant later.
5. The speaker started looking after some more plants.

A 1 and 2
B 2 and 3
C 4 and 5
D 2 and 4
E 3 and 5

20 "insects with mosaic wings" (line 36).
What does this tell you about the insects?

A The insects must be able to fly a very long way.
B The insects must have a great number of wings.
C The insects must all look exactly the same.
D The insects must be very colourful.
E The insects' bodies are boring to look at.

21 Why does the speaker give visitors "seeds and tools and gloves" (line 43)?

A So that more people will feel encouraged to visit the garden.
B So that they have something to remember their experience by.
C So that they can plant their own gardens.
D So that they will help the speaker to look after the garden.
E So that they will feel more hopeful when they return home.

22 Why is this poem called 'The Last Garden'?

A Because the speaker doesn't want to plant another garden.
B Because the speaker thinks people don't care enough to grow gardens.
C Because the speaker thinks no other gardens can grow.
D Because the speaker thinks theirs is the only garden in the world.
E Because the speaker thinks their garden will eventually perish.

23 Look at lines 1-24. How many leaves does the speaker's plant have to start with?

24 What was the screen built to protect the plant from?

25 Which one word in lines 21-24 means the same as 'hesitantly'?

26 Which three-word phrase in lines 37-40 means the same as 'many places'?

27 Which ONE part of speech are the following as they appear in the text?
in (line 2), on (line 15), Despite (line 24), from (line 29)

28 Which part of speech is 'gift' as it appears in the text? (line 43)

Turn over to the next page

Maths — Main Test

29 In a long jump competition, Noah's best jump measured 4.62 m and Olajide's best jump measured 3.78 m.

How much further did Noah jump than Olajide?

A 16 cm **B** 84 cm **C** 116 cm **D** 74 cm **E** 184 cm

---

30 Maggie goes to the shop to buy some glasses.
Small glasses come in boxes of 6. Large glasses come in boxes of 4.
She buys 5 boxes of small glasses and 3 boxes of large glasses.
On the journey back, 4 of the glasses crack. She throws these away.

How many glasses does Maggie have left?

A 42 **B** 38 **C** 12 **D** 30 **E** 48

---

31 Members of an art class were asked to choose their favourite type of paint.
The table shows the percentage of members that chose each type.

Favourite paint	Percentage of members
Acrylic	26%
Watercolour	30%
Oil	

There are 50 members in the art class.

How many members chose 'Oil'?

A 26 **B** 44 **C** 30 **D** 22 **E** 28

32 Moeen has a spinner with the numbers 1 to 5 on it.
He spins it once.

Which of the options below is the LEAST likely?

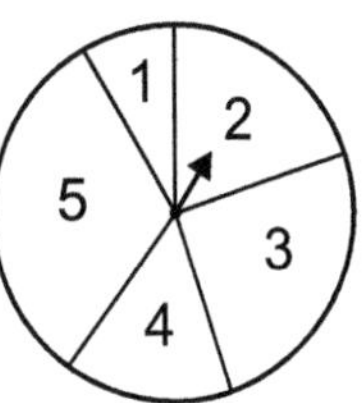

A   The arrow lands on 1.
B   The arrow lands on 2.
C   The arrow lands on either 3 or 4.
D   The arrow lands on either 1 or 5.
E   The arrow lands on 5.

---

33 Caoimhe wants to buy a gift for a friend.
She has £9.97 in her purse and £12.76 in a piggy bank.

Caoimhe sees a gift for £23 that she'd like to buy.

How much more money does Caoimhe need to buy the gift?

A   £3
B   21p
C   27p
D   £1.73
E   17p

---

34 **What time will a twenty-four hour clock show fifteen minutes before 10:02 pm?**

A   20:17
B   09:47
C   21:47
D   22:47
E   22:17

---

35 **What is $\frac{4}{25}$ as a decimal?**

A   0.4   B   0.16   C   0.2   D   0.04   E   0.25

Turn over to the next page

36 Five lines labelled **V**, **W**, **X**, **Y** and **Z** are shown below.

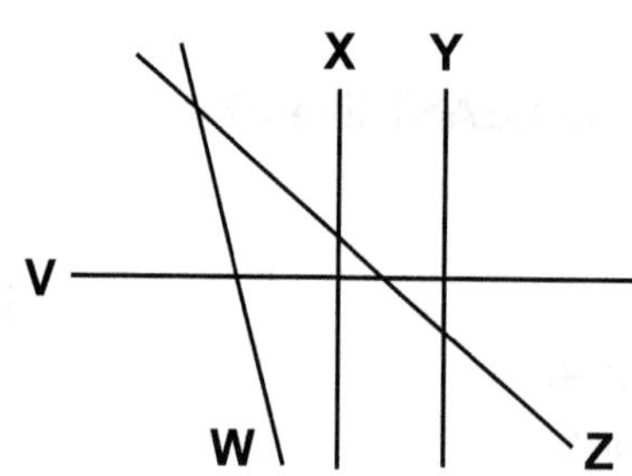

Which of the following statements is true?

A Y and Z are parallel.
B V and X are parallel.
C Z and X are perpendicular.
D None of the lines are parallel to each other.
E V and Y are perpendicular.

---

37 A cucumber weighs 380 g. A marrow is **10 times** heavier than the cucumber.

What is the weight of the marrow?

A 38 kg   **B** 3.8 kg   **C** 0.38 kg   **D** 380 kg   **E** 0.038 kg

---

38 A chessboard has 64 squares.
50% of the squares are white, and 50% are black.

Motsi paints 16 of the white squares black.

What percentage of the squares are coloured black now?

A 75%   **B** 66%   **C** 64%   **D** 48%   **E** 80%

39 The longer side of the rectangle below is twice the length of the shorter side.

3 cm

What is the perimeter of the rectangle?

A 12 cm   **B** 24 cm   **C** 9 cm   **D** 6 cm   **E** 18 cm

---

40 Below are the scheduled stops for a train travelling from Bursley to Foston.

Station	Bursley	Borwick	Grassbank	Lewton	Olby	Foston
Time	11:02	11:14	11:36	11:45	11:57	12:04

The train is 6 minutes late leaving Bursley.
It is also held up for 9 minutes between Grassbank and Lewton.

What time does the train leave Olby station?

A 11:57   **B** 12:15   **C** 12:03   **D** 12:12   **E** 12:19

---

41 The block graph shows the scores some children achieved in a maths test.

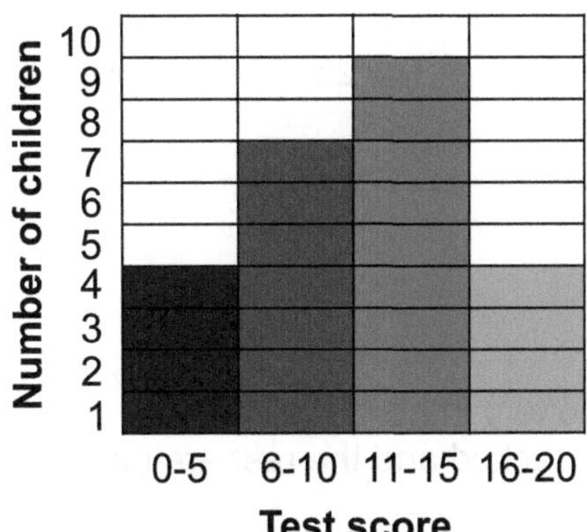

What fraction of the children scored between 16 and 20?

A ⅓   **B** ⅔   **C** ⅛   **D** ¼   **E** ⅙

Turn over to the next page

42 Saoirse buys three packets of crumpets.
The till display shows the total cost.

How much does one packet of crumpets cost?

A £1.20   B £1.50   C £1.40   D 14p   E £1.30

---

43 Look at this sequence of squares and triangles.

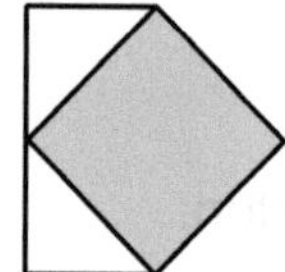
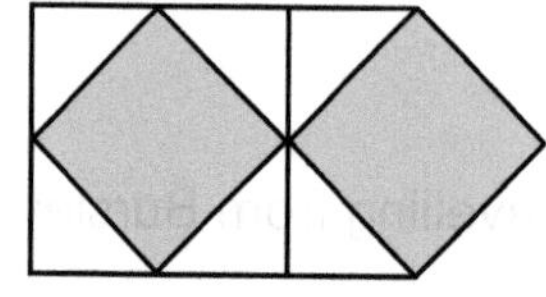
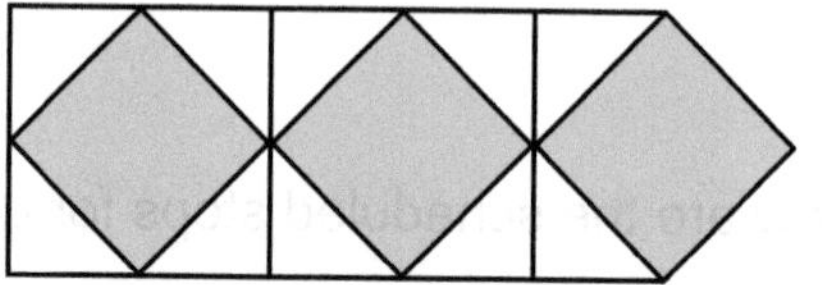

Pattern 1   **Pattern 2**   **Pattern 3**

What will be the total number of shapes in Pattern 7?

A 28   B 21   C 38   D 17   E 33

---

44 The table below shows 5 players' batting scores in a cricket match.

Name	Lorcan	Maura	Kim	Ricardo	Kehinde
Score	18	37	40	25	30

What is the mean score?

A 27   B 30   C 25   D 32   E 40

---

45 Akasha has 60 pieces of pottery in her collection.
$\frac{1}{5}$ of Akasha's pieces are cracked and the rest are undamaged.

How many pieces of undamaged pottery does Akasha have?

A 20   B 30   C 12   D 48   E 40

46 Conor has grown a flower. He measured the height of his flower
at the end of each week for 8 weeks and recorded the results in this table.

Time (weeks)	1	2	3	4	5	6	7	8
Height (cm)	2	3	6	12	14	17	18	20

Conor then plotted this line graph using the results from his table.

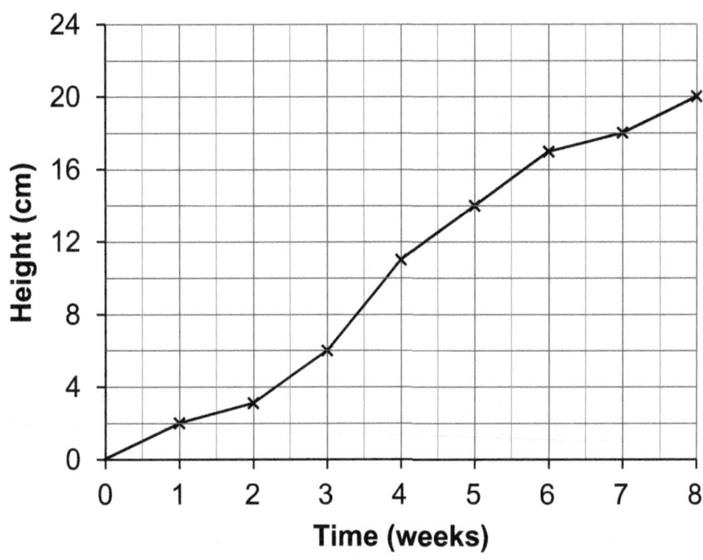

Which point has Conor plotted incorrectly?

A Week 5   **B** Week 4   **C** Week 6   **D** Week 3   **E** Week 8

---

47 **Which of these shapes has exactly 3 acute angles?**

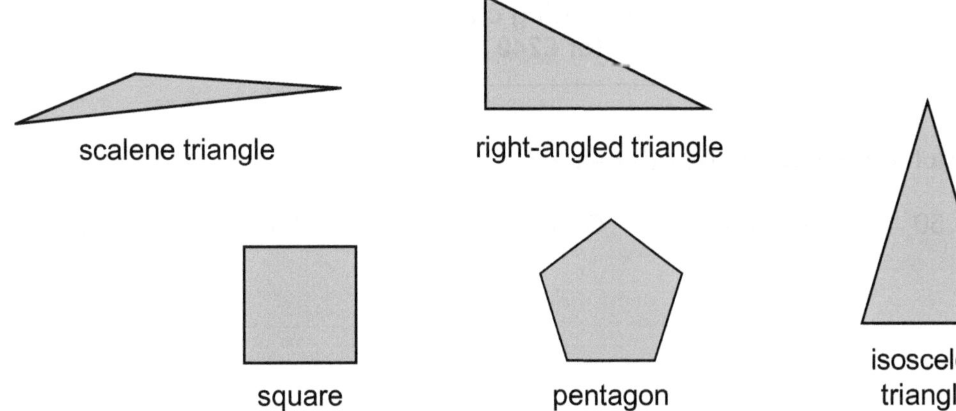

A scalene triangle
B right-angled triangle
C square
D pentagon
E isosceles triangle

Turn over to the next page

48 The grey triangle is reflected in the mirror line on this coordinate grid.

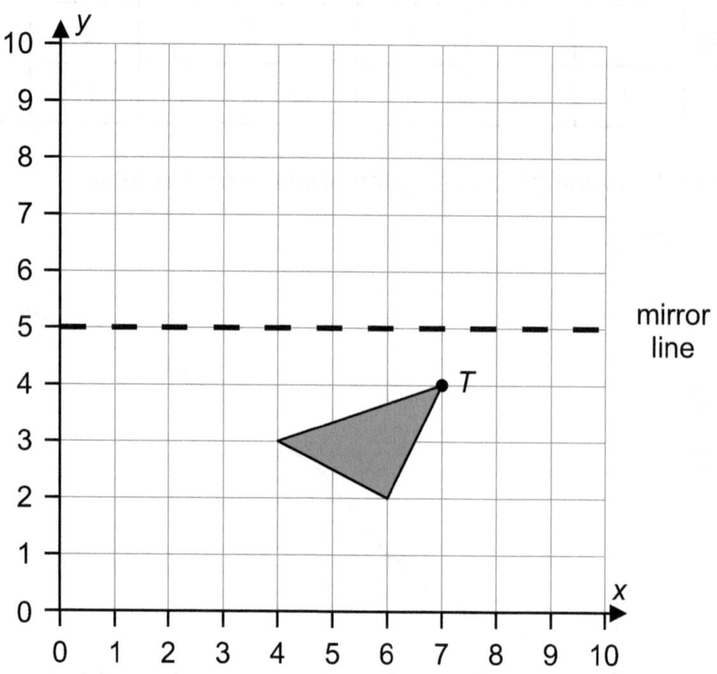

What are the coordinates of the reflection of point _T_?

A (4, 7)   **B** (6, 7)   **C** (7, 5)   **D** (7, 7)   **E** (7, 6)

---

49 A furniture shop sells dining chairs for £62.25 each.
The furniture shop has a special offer on:

SPECIAL OFFER
Buy 4 dining chairs
for £240

How much money does the offer save?

A £10.50   **B** £4.50   **C** £9   **D** £7.50   **E** £2.25

---

50 Gordon takes a cake out of the oven.
He measures the temperature as 66 °C, and decides to let the cake cool for a while.
When he measures the temperature later, it has **halved** and dropped by a further 15 °C.
Gordon then serves the cake.

What temperature is the cake when it is served?

A 18 °C   **B** 33 °C   **C** 30 °C   **D** 16 °C   **E** 20 °C

For the following questions, write your answers in the boxes provided on your answer sheet.
Any units needed are given on the answer sheet.

51   This is an isosceles triangle. The angles inside a triangle add up to 180°.

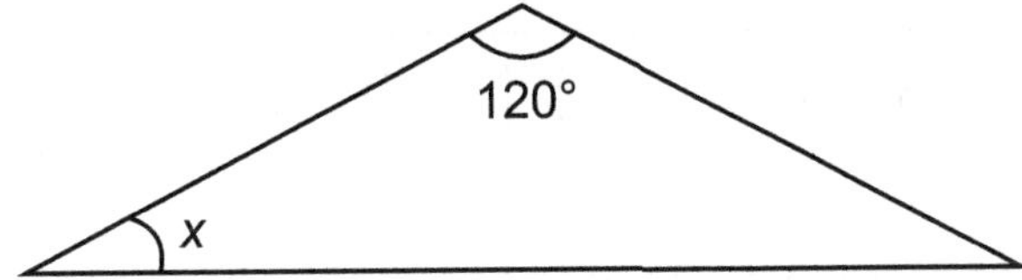

What is the size of angle x?

---

52   This is an empty picture frame.

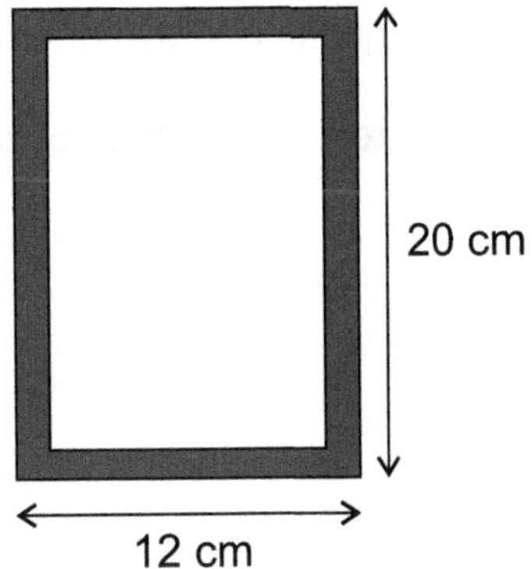

The area of the empty space within the frame is 195 cm².

What is the area of the grey frame?

---

53   There are 60 seconds in 1 minute.

How many seconds are there in 7 and a half minutes?

Turn over to the next page

54 The tally chart shows how many times rock, paper and scissors
were played in a rock, paper, scissors tournament.

Rock	JHT IIII
Paper	JHT II
Scissors	JHT JHT IIII

What percentage of plays were 'Rock'?

---

55 Tomi needs some milk for his breakfast.
He opens a new 2-litre bottle of milk and pours 178 ml of it onto his cereal.
He then pours another 22 ml of milk into a cup of coffee.

How many LITRES of milk are left in the milk bottle?

---

56 Sachiko makes a shape out of blocks.
Each block is a cube with a volume of 8 cm^3.

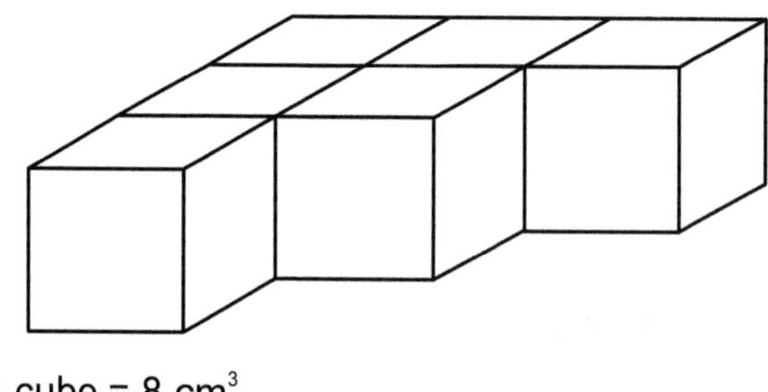

1 cube = 8 cm^3

What is the volume of the shape?

End of test

SEAG
Practice Papers

For the Entrance Assessment / Transfer Test

Answer Sheets

Using the Answer Sheets

The Entrance Assessment papers use special answer sheets like the ones in this booklet.

There's an answer sheet to go with each Practice Paper, so make sure you're filling in the right one. If you get used to these answer sheets now, it means there'll be no nasty surprises when you sit the real test.

Here are a few tips for using the answer sheets without getting yourself in a pickle...

Tips for Filling in the Answer Sheets

1) Before you start, fill in your name and the name of your school in the correct space. There may be boxes for other information, like your date of birth or your candidate number. Make sure you don't leave anything blank by mistake.

2) To mark your answer, put a clear pencil line in the answer box.

3) Make sure you have a pencil sharpener and an eraser for any mistakes.

4) If you make a mistake, rub out the incorrect answer first, and then fill in your new answer clearly.

5) It's easy to lose your place when you move from the test paper to the answer sheet, so match up the question number on the paper and the answer sheet. Keeping the two sheets close together will help you do this.

6) If you skip a question to come back to later, make sure you leave a gap for that question on the answer sheet. That way your answers will stay in order.

7) Don't do working out on your answer sheet.

8) Don't worry if you mark boxes in the same position several times in a row — just because you've marked the second box four times, it doesn't mean that your answers are wrong.

Practice Paper — Set A: Paper 1

Candidate's name:

School name:

Date of Test		
Day	Month	Year

Date of Birth		
Day	Month	Year

Candidate Number

School Number

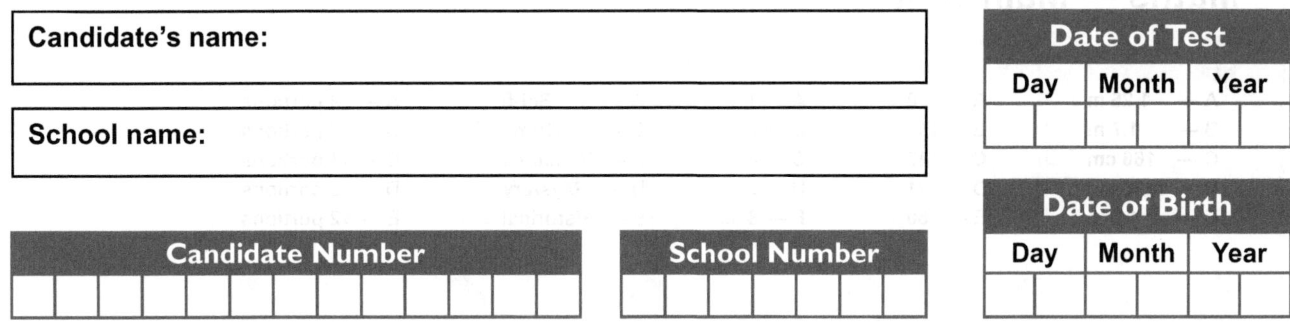

English — Practice Test

P1 A B C D N

P2 A B C D E

P3 A B C D N

P4 A B C D E

P5

Maths — Practice Test

P6
A — Cormac
B — Maria
C — Liam
D — Rowan
E — Elise

P7
A — 5
B — 14
C — 9
D — 11
E — 15

P8
A — 8
B — 9
C — 7
D — 5
E — 6

P9 ________ vertices

P10 ________ children

English — Main Test

1 A B C D N

2 A B C D N

3 A B C D N

4 A B C D N

5 A B C D N

6 A B C D E

7 A B C D E

8 A B C D E

9 A B C D E

10 A B C D E

11 A B C D N

12 A B C D N

13 A B C D N

14 A B C D N

15 A B C D N

16 A B C D E

17 A B C D E

18 A B C D E

19 A B C D E

20 A B C D E

21 A B C D E

22 A B C D E

23

24

25

26

27

28

Maths — Main Test

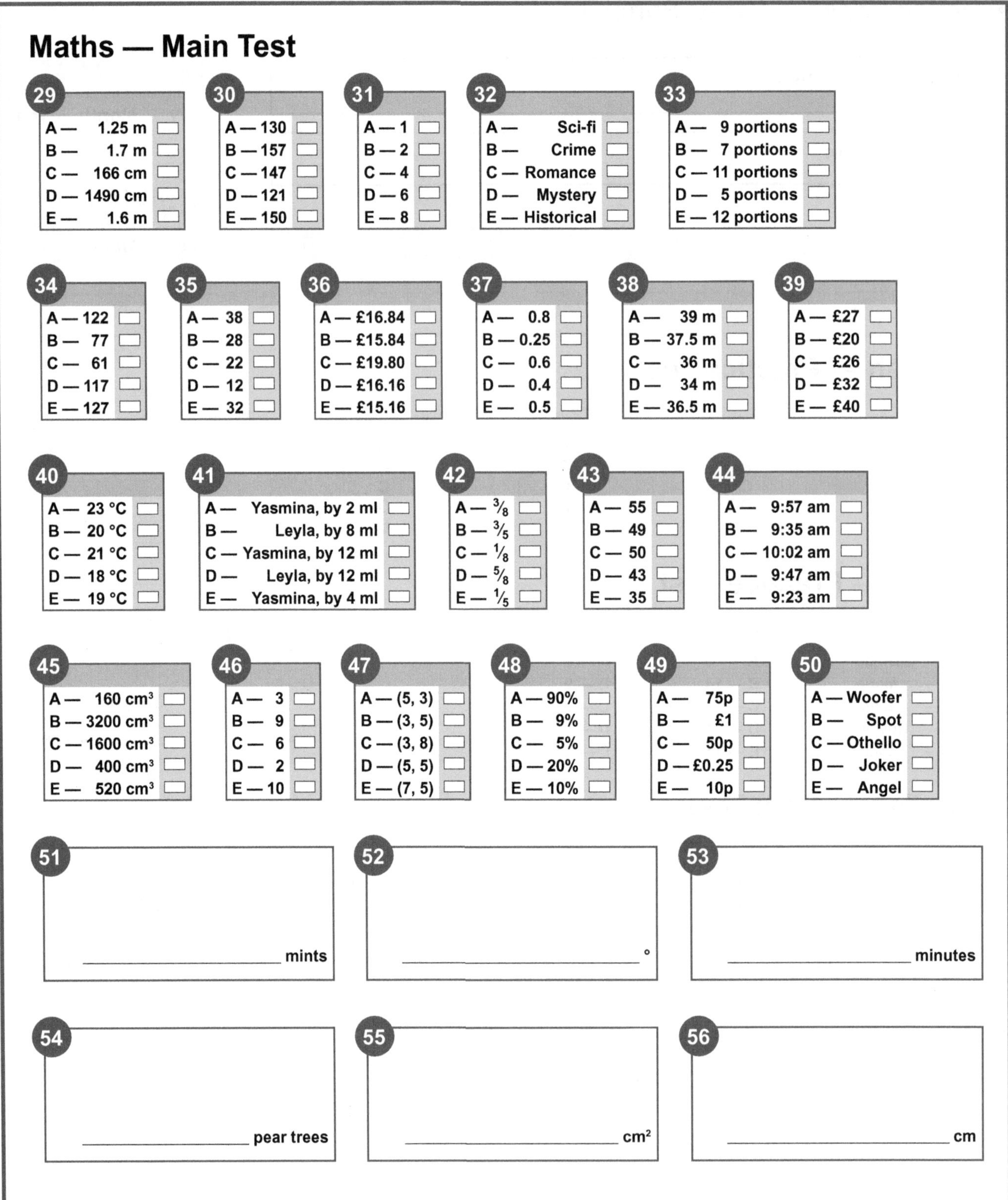

29
A — 1.25 m
B — 1.7 m
C — 166 cm
D — 1490 cm
E — 1.6 m

30
A — 130
B — 157
C — 147
D — 121
E — 150

31
A — 1
B — 2
C — 4
D — 6
E — 8

32
A — Sci-fi
B — Crime
C — Romance
D — Mystery
E — Historical

33
A — 9 portions
B — 7 portions
C — 11 portions
D — 5 portions
E — 12 portions

34
A — 122
B — 77
C — 61
D — 117
E — 127

35
A — 38
B — 28
C — 22
D — 12
E — 32

36
A — £16.84
B — £15.84
C — £19.80
D — £16.16
E — £15.16

37
A — 0.8
B — 0.25
C — 0.6
D — 0.4
E — 0.5

38
A — 39 m
B — 37.5 m
C — 36 m
D — 34 m
E — 36.5 m

39
A — £27
B — £20
C — £26
D — £32
E — £40

40
A — 23 °C
B — 20 °C
C — 21 °C
D — 18 °C
E — 19 °C

41
A — Yasmina, by 2 ml
B — Leyla, by 8 ml
C — Yasmina, by 12 ml
D — Leyla, by 12 ml
E — Yasmina, by 4 ml

42
A — $\frac{3}{8}$
B — $\frac{3}{5}$
C — $\frac{1}{8}$
D — $\frac{5}{8}$
E — $\frac{1}{5}$

43
A — 55
B — 49
C — 50
D — 43
E — 35

44
A — 9:57 am
B — 9:35 am
C — 10:02 am
D — 9:47 am
E — 9:23 am

45
A — 160 cm³
B — 3200 cm³
C — 1600 cm³
D — 400 cm³
E — 520 cm³

46
A — 3
B — 9
C — 6
D — 2
E — 10

47
A — (5, 3)
B — (3, 5)
C — (3, 8)
D — (5, 5)
E — (7, 5)

48
A — 90%
B — 9%
C — 5%
D — 20%
E — 10%

49
A — 75p
B — £1
C — 50p
D — £0.25
E — 10p

50
A — Woofer
B — Spot
C — Othello
D — Joker
E — Angel

51
________________ mints

52
________________ °

53
________________ minutes

54
________________ pear trees

55
________________ cm²

56
________________ cm

Practice Paper — Set A: Paper 2

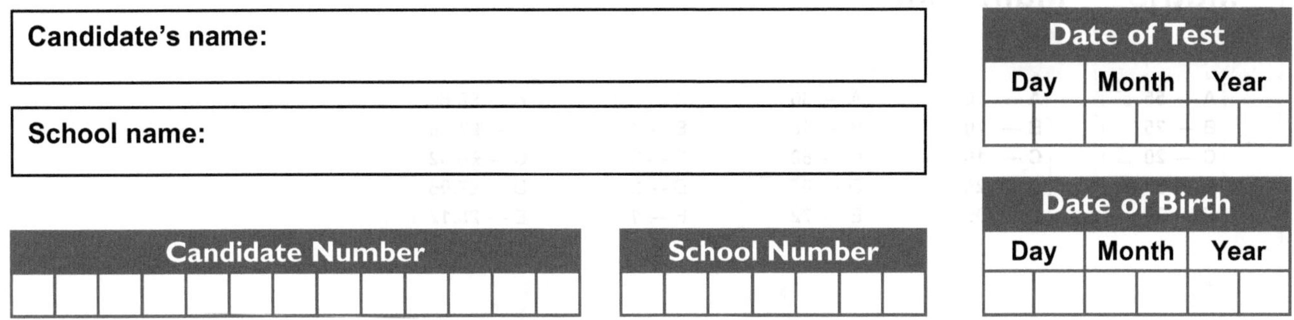

English — Practice Test

P1	P2	P3	P4	P5
A B C D N	A B C D E	A B C D N	A B C D E	

Maths — Practice Test

P6	P7	P8	P9	P10
A — Mug B — Cap C — Scarf D — Poster E — T-shirt	A — 12 B — 5 C — 6 D — 8 E — 10	A — 287 B — 345 C — 249 D — 256 E — 329	______ m	______ %

English — Main Test

1	2	3	4	5	6	7	8	9	10
A B C D N	A B C D N	A B C D N	A B C D N	A B C D N	A B C D E	A B C D E	A B C D E	A B C D E	A B C D E

11	12	13	14	15	16	17	18	19	20
A B C D N	A B C D N	A B C D N	A B C D N	A B C D N	A B C D E	A B C D E	A B C D E	A B C D E	A B C D E

21	22	23	24	25
A B C D E	A B C D E			

26	27	28

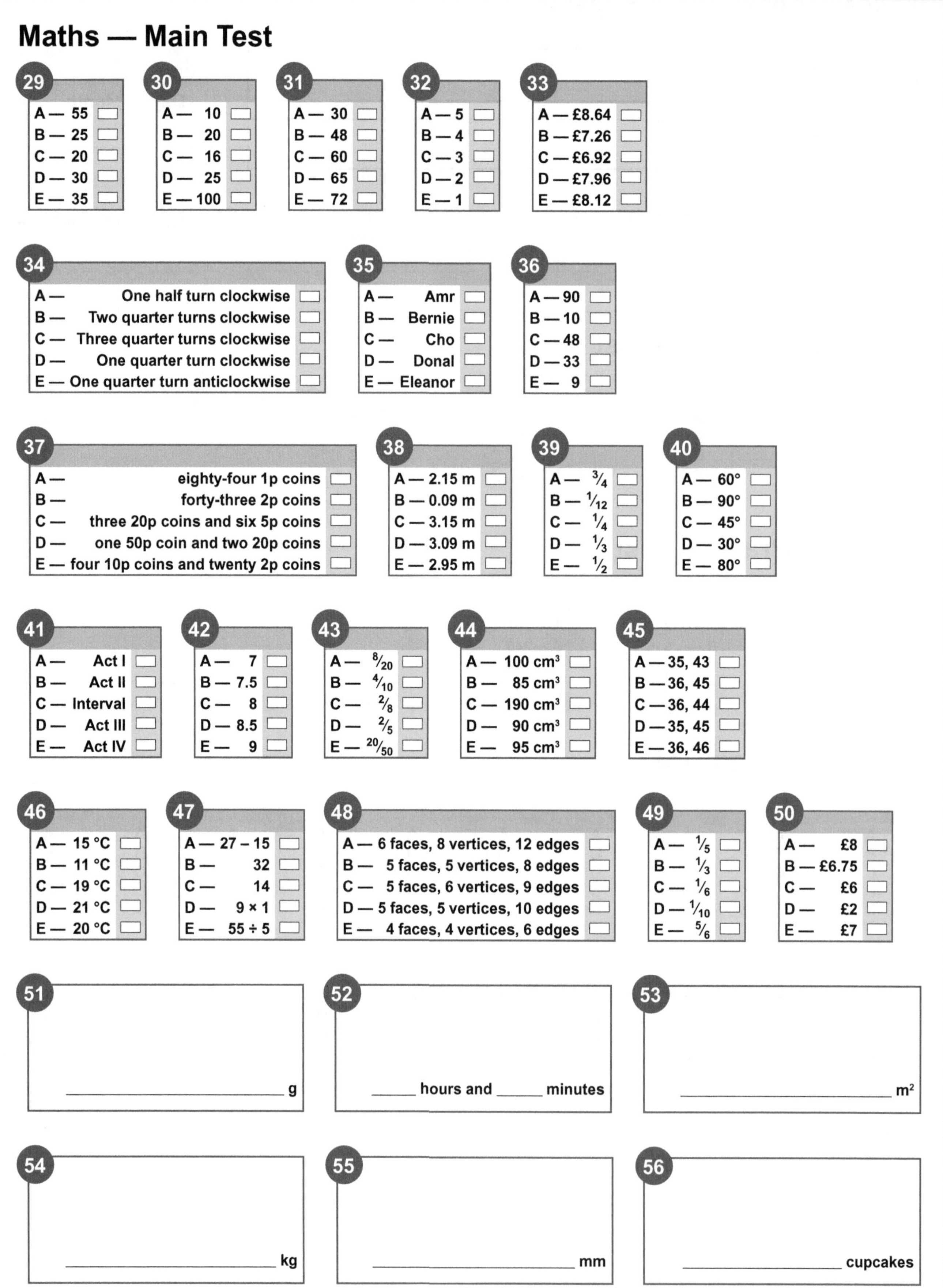

29
A — 55
B — 25
C — 20
D — 30
E — 35

30
A — 10
B — 20
C — 16
D — 25
E — 100

31
A — 30
B — 48
C — 60
D — 65
E — 72

32
A — 5
B — 4
C — 3
D — 2
E — 1

33
A — £8.64
B — £7.26
C — £6.92
D — £7.96
E — £8.12

34
A — One half turn clockwise
B — Two quarter turns clockwise
C — Three quarter turns clockwise
D — One quarter turn clockwise
E — One quarter turn anticlockwise

35
A — Amr
B — Bernie
C — Cho
D — Donal
E — Eleanor

36
A — 90
B — 10
C — 48
D — 33
E — 9

37
A — eighty-four 1p coins
B — forty-three 2p coins
C — three 20p coins and six 5p coins
D — one 50p coin and two 20p coins
E — four 10p coins and twenty 2p coins

38
A — 2.15 m
B — 0.09 m
C — 3.15 m
D — 3.09 m
E — 2.95 m

39
A — $\frac{3}{4}$
B — $\frac{1}{12}$
C — $\frac{1}{4}$
D — $\frac{1}{3}$
E — $\frac{1}{2}$

40
A — 60°
B — 90°
C — 45°
D — 30°
E — 80°

41
A — Act I
B — Act II
C — Interval
D — Act III
E — Act IV

42
A — 7
B — 7.5
C — 8
D — 8.5
E — 9

43
A — $\frac{8}{20}$
B — $\frac{4}{10}$
C — $\frac{2}{8}$
D — $\frac{2}{5}$
E — $\frac{20}{50}$

44
A — 100 cm³
B — 85 cm³
C — 190 cm³
D — 90 cm³
E — 95 cm³

45
A — 35, 43
B — 36, 45
C — 36, 44
D — 35, 45
E — 36, 46

46
A — 15 °C
B — 11 °C
C — 19 °C
D — 21 °C
E — 20 °C

47
A — 27 − 15
B — 32
C — 14
D — 9 × 1
E — 55 ÷ 5

48
A — 6 faces, 8 vertices, 12 edges
B — 5 faces, 5 vertices, 8 edges
C — 5 faces, 6 vertices, 9 edges
D — 5 faces, 5 vertices, 10 edges
E — 4 faces, 4 vertices, 6 edges

49
A — $\frac{1}{5}$
B — $\frac{1}{3}$
C — $\frac{1}{6}$
D — $\frac{1}{10}$
E — $\frac{5}{6}$

50
A — £8
B — £6.75
C — £6
D — £2
E — £7

51
__________________ g

52
______ hours and ______ minutes

53
__________________ m²

54
__________________ kg

55
__________________ mm

56
__________________ cupcakes

Practice Paper — Set B: Paper 1

Candidate's name:

School name:

Date of Test

Day	Month	Year

Date of Birth

Day	Month	Year

Candidate Number

School Number

English — Practice Test

P1 — A B C D N

P2 — A B C D E

P3 — A B C D N

P4 — A B C D E

P5

Maths — Practice Test

P6
- A — 30p
- B — 50p
- C — 80p
- D — 70p
- E — 60p

P7
- A — Blue
- B — Black
- C — White
- D — Red
- E — Silver

P8
- A — 1
- B — 2
- C — 3
- D — 4
- E — 6

P9 ______ m

P10 ______ people

English — Main Test

1 — A B C D N

2 — A B C D N

3 — A B C D N

4 — A B C D N

5 — A B C D N

6 — A B C D E

7 — A B C D E

8 — A B C D E

9 — A B C D E

10 — A B C D E

11 — A B C D N

12 — A B C D N

13 — A B C D N

14 — A B C D N

15 — A B C D N

16 — A B C D E

17 — A B C D E

18 — A B C D E

19 — A B C D E

20 — A B C D E

21 — A B C D E

22 — A B C D E

23

24

25

26

27

28

Maths — Main Test

29
A — 10 s
B — 30 s
C — 25 s
D — 17 s
E — 3 s

30
A — It has four lines of symmetry.
B — It doesn't have any right angles.
C — All of its angles are different.
D — It has two pairs of equal-length sides.
E — All of its sides are the same length.

31
A — 15:19
B — 16:33
C — 15:33
D — 15:17
E — 15:05

32
A — 30%
B — $\frac{1}{3}$
C — $\frac{3}{10}$
D — 0.3
E — $\frac{30}{100}$

33
A — Cylinder
B — Cuboid
C — Square-based pyramid
D — Cone
E — Triangular prism

34
A — 128 minutes
B — 1 hour and 12 minutes
C — 1 hour and 36 minutes
D — 112 minutes
E — 54 minutes

35
A — £5.14
B — £4.26
C — £4.86
D — £5.24
E — £5.54

36
A — $\frac{4}{10}$
B — $\frac{3}{10}$
C — $\frac{1}{4}$
D — $\frac{3}{20}$
E — $\frac{1}{5}$

37
A — 30
B — 18
C — 49
D — 17
E — 34

38
A — 216
B — 162
C — 92
D — 108
E — 90

39
A — 50 km
B — 12.5 km
C — 5 km
D — 15 km
E — 25 km

40
A — 100
B — 36
C — 49
D — 56
E — 121

41
A — (2, 11)
B — (0, 7)
C — (10, 7)
D — (5, 0)
E — (11, 7)

42
A — 1 kg
B — 0.2 kg
C — 1.5 kg
D — 0.5 kg
E — 2 kg

43
A — 0:45
B — 1:30
C — 2:15
D — 1:15
E — 1:20

44
A — 300.2
B — 3200
C — 3002
D — 302
E — 3020

45
A — 65%
B — 85%
C — 50%
D — 75%
E — 90%

46
A — 46
B — 23
C — 40
D — 32
E — 43

47
A — 42
B — 64
C — 84
D — 56
E — 72

48
A — Prisha, by 1 cm
B — Raj, by 3 cm
C — Prisha, by 5 cm
D — Raj, by 7 cm
E — Prisha, by 14 cm

49
A — £31.00
B — £33.50
C — £28.50
D — £36.00
E — £26.00

50
A — 4.9 kg
B — 4750 g
C — 475 g
D — 4.8 kg
E — 4.5 kg

51
__________ cm²

52
______ minutes and ______ seconds

53
£ __________

54
__________ g

55
__________ months

56
__________ cm

Practice Paper — Set B: Paper 2

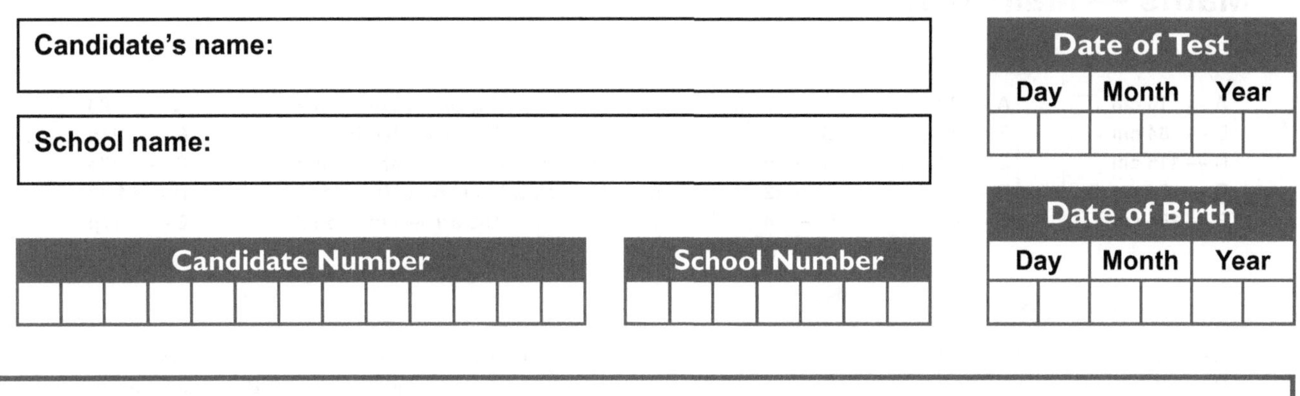

English — Practice Test

P1 A B C D N

P2 A B C D E

P3 A B C D N

P4 A B C D E

P5

Maths — Practice Test

P6
A — 3:30
B — 2:45
C — 3:45
D — 2:15
E — 2:30

P7
A — 350 g
B — 400 g
C — 150 g
D — 100 g
E — 250 g

P8
A — $\frac{1}{2}$
B — $\frac{3}{5}$
C — $\frac{2}{5}$
D — $\frac{2}{3}$
E — $\frac{3}{4}$

P9 ______ Labradors

P10 ______ children

English — Main Test

1 A B C D N
2 A B C D N
3 A B C D N
4 A B C D N
5 A B C D N
6 A B C D E
7 A B C D E
8 A B C D E
9 A B C D E
10 A B C D E

11 A B C D N
12 A B C D N
13 A B C D N
14 A B C D N
15 A B C D N
16 A B C D E
17 A B C D E
18 A B C D E
19 A B C D E
20 A B C D E

21 A B C D E
22 A B C D E
23
24
25
26
27
28

Maths — Main Test

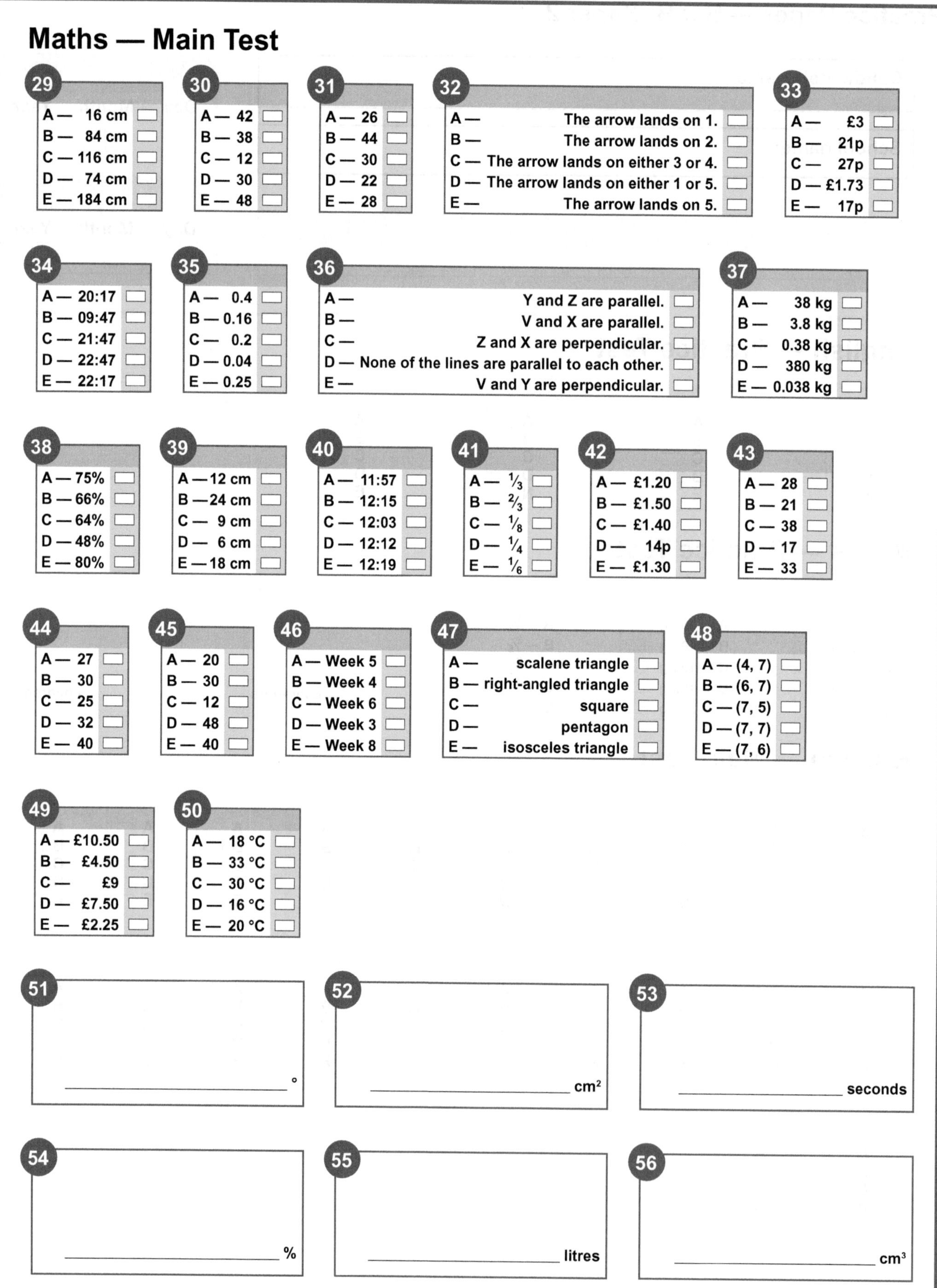

29
- A — 16 cm
- B — 84 cm
- C — 116 cm
- D — 74 cm
- E — 184 cm

30
- A — 42
- B — 38
- C — 12
- D — 30
- E — 48

31
- A — 26
- B — 44
- C — 30
- D — 22
- E — 28

32
- A — The arrow lands on 1.
- B — The arrow lands on 2.
- C — The arrow lands on either 3 or 4.
- D — The arrow lands on either 1 or 5.
- E — The arrow lands on 5.

33
- A — £3
- B — 21p
- C — 27p
- D — £1.73
- E — 17p

34
- A — 20:17
- B — 09:47
- C — 21:47
- D — 22:47
- E — 22:17

35
- A — 0.4
- B — 0.16
- C — 0.2
- D — 0.04
- E — 0.25

36
- A — Y and Z are parallel.
- B — V and X are parallel.
- C — Z and X are perpendicular.
- D — None of the lines are parallel to each other.
- E — V and Y are perpendicular.

37
- A — 38 kg
- B — 3.8 kg
- C — 0.38 kg
- D — 380 kg
- E — 0.038 kg

38
- A — 75%
- B — 66%
- C — 64%
- D — 48%
- E — 80%

39
- A — 12 cm
- B — 24 cm
- C — 9 cm
- D — 6 cm
- E — 18 cm

40
- A — 11:57
- B — 12:15
- C — 12:03
- D — 12:12
- E — 12:19

41
- A — $\frac{1}{3}$
- B — $\frac{2}{3}$
- C — $\frac{1}{8}$
- D — $\frac{1}{4}$
- E — $\frac{1}{6}$

42
- A — £1.20
- B — £1.50
- C — £1.40
- D — 14p
- E — £1.30

43
- A — 28
- B — 21
- C — 38
- D — 17
- E — 33

44
- A — 27
- B — 30
- C — 25
- D — 32
- E — 40

45
- A — 20
- B — 30
- C — 12
- D — 48
- E — 40

46
- A — Week 5
- B — Week 4
- C — Week 6
- D — Week 3
- E — Week 8

47
- A — scalene triangle
- B — right-angled triangle
- C — square
- D — pentagon
- E — isosceles triangle

48
- A — (4, 7)
- B — (6, 7)
- C — (7, 5)
- D — (7, 7)
- E — (7, 6)

49
- A — £10.50
- B — £4.50
- C — £9
- D — £7.50
- E — £2.25

50
- A — 18 °C
- B — 33 °C
- C — 30 °C
- D — 16 °C
- E — 20 °C

51 _____________ °

52 _____________ cm²

53 _____________ seconds

54 _____________ %

55 _____________ litres

56 _____________ cm³

BLANK PAGE

SEAG
Practice Papers

For the Entrance Assessment / Transfer Test

Answer Book &
Parents' Guide

Published by CGP

Editors:
Aimee Ashurst, Emma Crighton, Emma Duffee, Jake McGuffie,
Caley Simpson, Matt Topping and Maddie Wright.

Many thanks to Gill Bowmer, Becca Clifford and Ali Palin for the proofreading.

With thanks to Jan Greenway for the copyright research.
With thanks to Hannah Fishwick for the audio recording.

ISBN: 978 1 83774 101 4

Printed by Elanders Ltd, Newcastle upon Tyne.
Clipart from Corel®

What this pack contains

This pack contains **two sets** of Practice Papers for the Entrance Assessment set by SEAG.

The questions in these papers have been written to match the level of difficulty of the real exam. They are designed to test your child's English and Maths skills.

Each of the practice papers in this pack has an accompanying **answer sheet**, just like the answer sheets used in the real exams. There are also **full answers** to every question in this booklet.

The pages that follow in this **Parents' Guide** are designed to give some guidance on how to best prepare for the Entrance Assessment, as well as how to support your child in performing as well as they can.

Online Audio

You can also download and play the **online audio instructions**. These instruct your child when to begin and end the test, using the same timings as the real exam. They also give an introduction to the test and explain how the test works.

You can find the audio downloads by following the link or scanning the QR code:

cgpbooks.co.uk/SEAGtestaudio

This set of papers also includes a **free Online Edition**. For details of how to access your Online Edition, just follow the instructions in the box below:

Unlock your Online Edition

Just scan the QR code below or go to **cgpbooks.co.uk/extras** and enter this code!

2990 5811 4475 4805

By the way, this code only works for one person. If somebody else has used this book before you, they might have already claimed the code.

- It's important to remember that preparing to take the test can be a stressful time for both parents and pupils. You should do all you can to minimise pressure for the whole family, and try to make the whole process as positive an experience as possible.
- When studying for the test, your child will learn plenty of new skills that can have a beneficial impact on their whole education, regardless of whether they pass the test.
- With the right mindset and preparation, your child will be able to approach the test with confidence, and come out of it feeling positive about their performance.

This page covers the basics — what the Entrance Assessment is and how it works.

The Entrance Assessment is a selective test

Most secondary schools in Northern Ireland are comprehensive — they accept children of all abilities. However, some selective schools (grammar schools) choose their pupils based on academic ability.

The Entrance Assessment is used to determine if a child is suitable for grammar school. Children usually sit the test in the first term of their last year at primary school.

The structure of the test

The Entrance Assessment is set by **SEAG** and **GL Assessment**. There are **two papers** in total — both papers have the same structure and format, but they are usually taken two weeks apart.

Some questions are **multiple choice**, while others are **free response**:

> **Multiple choice** — there's a choice of five options for each answer.
>
> **Free response** — there are spaces on the Answer Sheet for the pupil to write their own answers. There won't be any answer options given for the pupil to choose from.

Each paper is split into three sections:
Practice Test, **English Main Test** and **Maths Main Test**.

> **Practice Test**
> - English Practice Test — 1 question each on punctuation, grammar and spelling. Then a short passage with 2 comprehension questions (1 multiple choice, 1 free response).
> - Maths Practice Test — 3 multiple choice questions, 2 free response questions.
>
> This section is **not assessed** — it's there to help pupils settle in before the Main Test begins.

> **English Main Test**
> Punctuation Exercise — 5 multiple choice questions.
> Grammar Exercise — 5 multiple choice questions.
> Spelling Exercise — 5 multiple choice questions.
> Comprehension Exercise — 13 questions (7 multiple choice and 6 free response).

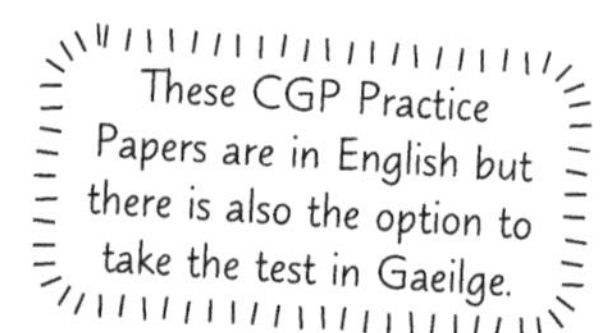

> **Maths Main Test**
> 22 multiple choice questions followed by 6 free response questions.

If you want to use the Practice Papers under timed exam-style conditions, allow your child **60 minutes** to complete the 56 questions in the English and Maths Main Tests. The two Main Tests can be completed in either order, but pupils should spend roughly **30 minutes** on each. The Practice Test does not need to be timed.

The Statement of Outcomes

After the tests, your child's '**raw score**' (the actual number of questions they answered correctly) will be converted into a '**standardised score**', which takes into account your child's age when they take the test.

You will receive a **Statement of Outcomes** containing standardised scores for **both** Main Tests, a **Total Standardised Age Score** (the **TSAS**) and the **Band** (1-6) this score puts your child in. Schools also receive this data, and will use some or all of it when deciding whether to award your child a place.

Using the Practice Papers

This advice will help you to get the most out of this set of practice papers. You may wish to administer the practice papers in exam conditions to help your child become familiar with the format of the test.

Most answers are in multiple choice format

There is advice on filling in the answer sheets on page 2 of the answer sheet booklet. Read through this advice with your child before you begin. Make sure that they understand what they need to do before they begin a paper, and that they are filling in the answer sheet which matches the paper they are attempting.

How to set the practice papers

- Do the practice papers at a time when your child usually works well. This might be a weekday after school, or at the weekend. This will help them work to the best of their abilities.
- As you get closer to the actual test, it is a good idea to sit some practice papers at the same time of day as the real thing — that way, your child will be used to the routine and there shouldn't be any surprises.
- Your child should attempt the practice paper at a clear table in a quiet area, free from distractions and interruptions.
- They'll need a sharp HB pencil, an eraser and a pencil sharpener, plus a blank page for their working out.
- You can play the online audio to create realistic exam conditions. The audio will give your child instructions for answering the paper, as well as information about timings.
- Position your child so they can see a watch or clock so that they can keep track of the time they have left.
- Give your child as much time as they need to work on the Practice Questions at the start of each paper.
- Time the main part of the test strictly. If they haven't finished the paper in the time allowed, you could draw a line under the last question they answered within the time limit so you know to give marks up to that point. You can then time them to see how long it takes them to finish the paper. This will allow you to monitor the speed your child is working at.
- Encourage them to read over their answers if they finish within the time limit, but don't give them extra time to do this.
- Mark their test using the answers in this booklet.

Marking the practice papers

You should give one mark for each correct answer your child gave within the time limit, then work out the total score. It's really important to go through any wrong answers with your child — use the explanations in the answer book to show them how to find the right answer.

The pass mark for the Entrance Assessment will vary from year to year. As such, there is no number of correct answers that will guarantee a pass.

However, your child's score might help you pinpoint specific skills that they need to practise. For example, if your child scored 60%, got nearly all the questions right, but didn't finish the test, they need to work faster. We have given some advice to help you increase your child's speed on p.6.

If they scored 60%, got to the end, but got 40% of the questions wrong, they need to brush up on their accuracy. You can follow this up with some more practice in the areas they struggled with, then set another practice test.

Improving Your Child's Score

For your child to do well in their test, they'll need to work quickly and avoid making mistakes.
Here's some advice to help improve your child's score and test technique.

Start by working on accuracy...

When your child is just starting out, it's a good idea to focus on their accuracy and understanding,
rather than speed. You can work on their speed when they're a bit more confident.

Once your child has finished a paper and you've marked it, you should go over the questions
they got wrong, so they know how they should have answered them. You could even come back
to these trickier questions at a later date to make sure they can still get them right.

...then work on speed

It's important that children are able to answer questions under time pressure.

Once your child can accurately answer Entrance Assessment questions,
use these tips to help them improve their speed:

> * When they're practising, give your child slightly less time than the real test to do the
>   same number of questions.
> * Encourage your child only to check their answers at the end of the test.
> * You could introduce games to get them working faster — try using a stopwatch to time a
>   set of questions, and get your child to ring a bell or shout when they've finished them.
> * For comprehension questions, it's important that your child can read the text quickly.
>   Encourage them to read the text first, then look at the questions — remind them that
>   they can look back at the text as many times as they like when answering the questions.

In the run-up to the test, start working on test technique

Your child will score better on the Entrance Assessment if they improve their test technique. Good test
technique is also important for other exams later in their education. When they start working through
assessment papers, remind them to do the following things:

> * Read the question carefully to avoid silly mistakes.
> * Skip any questions that are really difficult, or which are taking a long time
>   — they can come back to them if there's time at the end.
> * If they can't do a question and they're running out of time, make a sensible guess.
>   For multiple choice questions, they may be able to rule out one or two options that definitely
>   aren't correct, which gives a better chance of guessing which of the remaining ones is right.

For questions in multiple choice format, there are some other specific techniques to practise:

> * Marking the correct box neatly and quickly using a horizontal line.
> * Making sure they mark the answer in the correct box, especially if they skip a question.
> * If they don't finish the paper, filling in the rest of the answers randomly.

When your child does a practice paper, they should work in silence and without help.
Try to make their experience as close to the real test as possible.

The test days and the time before you get the results can be just as stressful for you as for your child. Here are some tips about how to reduce this stress, and how to cope with the waiting period.

Facing the test

Make sure you and your child are fully prepared for the day of the test. You need to know:

- Where the test is and how you're going to get there (parking may be difficult).
- What time the test starts and what time you need to arrive by.
- What they'll need to take (pencils, etc.) or whether everything is provided for them.

Make sure your child is as relaxed as possible the night before the test, and that they get a good night's sleep. A healthy evening meal and breakfast before the test will also help put your child in the right frame of mind to tackle the test. It's also a good idea to talk them through the arrangements for the day so they know what will happen.

After the test, plan an outing or a treat which will take your child's (and your) mind off the test.

- Let the test centre know as soon as possible if you can't make it to one of the test days.
- There won't be an opportunity to retake any part of the test. If your child only takes one of the two papers, they'll be given an estimated overall score.
- If you think there are circumstances that have affected your child's performance in the test, gather evidence of this as soon as possible (e.g. a doctor's note).

After the Entrance Assessment

Make a plan for the time between the last of your child's tests and the day you get their results — this wait can be stressful.

If you're going to reward your child for their hard work preparing for the Entrance Assessment, you might want to do it now. If they're rewarded for their effort and hard work, they'll realise that they've achieved something, even if their results aren't what they hoped for.

Remind your child that you are proud of them no matter what the outcome, and try not to build up results day as too big a deal. If your child is unsuccessful, then it's not the end of the world. If your child does gain a grammar school place, then make sure they're aware that some of their classmates might not have done, and may need a friend to help make them feel better.

If you feel there is good reason, then this is also a good time to research the appeals process for the schools you've applied to. Some parents choose to appeal the admission decision if their child isn't offered a place.

Make sure you have an alternative plan

For some grammar schools, there can be several applicants for each available place. Even if your child scores highly on the test, it may still not be enough to gain a place at the school. You should put at least one non-selective school on your application form — it's a good idea to have visited these schools, so your child knows what to expect if they aren't offered a grammar school place.

It's important that your child doesn't feel like a failure if they don't get into a grammar school — there are many excellent non-selective schools where your child can be happy and successful. Remember that school is what you make it, and a positive response to not gaining a grammar school place is key to this.

Set A: Paper 1

English — Practice Test

Pages 2-3

P1) B
'madrid' should be 'Madrid' — it starts with a capital letter
because it is a proper noun.

P2) C
The possessive pronoun 'their' is correct as the students
all have the same teacher.

P3) D
'suspitious' should be 'suspicious' — the suffix is 'cious' not 'tious'.

P4) C
The text says that "his dad's car wouldn't start, meaning
he would have to get the bus to school" (lines 2-3).

P5) furiously
"furiously" (line 6) means the same as 'angrily'.

Maths — Practice Test

Pages 4-5

P6) C — Liam
Amani's birthday is the 22nd January. 5 days after this is the
27th January. Looking at the table, this is Liam's birthday,
so the answer is Liam.

P7) B — 14
They went on 5 hikes in February and 9 hikes in March,
which is 5 + 9 = 14 hikes in total.

P8) C — 7
There are 84 ÷ 12 = 7 chairs in each row.

P9) 6 vertices
A a triangular prism has 6 vertices, 5 faces and 9 edges.

P10) 27 children
$\frac{1}{4}$ of 36 = 36 ÷ 4 = 9 children play brass instruments,
so 36 − 9 = 27 children do not play brass instruments.

English — Main Test

Pages 6-12

1) B
There should be a closing bracket after 'Suzy',
as this is extra information.

2) B
'rose' should be 'Rose' — it starts with a capital letter
because it is a proper noun.

3) A
'hasnt' should be 'hasn't' — it needs an apostrophe
because it is a contraction of 'has not'.

4) C
'cat's' should be 'cats' — you don't add an apostrophe
to make something plural.

5) N
There are no mistakes in this line.

6) B
'despite' is correct — it is the preposition
that makes the most sense in this context.

7) B
'well' is correct because it is an adverb and the other options are adjectives.

8) C
'by' is correct — it is the only preposition that makes sense
in this sentence.

9) A
'she'll' is correct because it is a contraction of 'she will',
which is consistent with the tense of the rest of the sentence.

10) E
'which' is correct — it is the only option that makes sense in this sentence.

11) D
'specal' should be 'special'. The suffix is 'cial', not 'cal'.

12) B
'acommodation' should be 'accommodation'.
The word is spelt with a double 'c'.

13) D
'pours' should be 'pores' — 'pores' are small holes in the skin,
whereas 'pours' is a verb meaning 'causes liquid to flow'.

14) N
There are no mistakes in this line.

15) C
'tention' should be 'tension'. The suffix is 'sion', not 'tion'.

16) D
The text says that "it became important to keep track of more detailed
information" (line 9), so people developed the writing system that would
eventually become cuneiform.

17) C
The text says that a scribe "would press a stylus into the clay" (lines 17-18)
and that this was done when the clay was "moist" (line 17).
This means statements 1 and 4 are correct.

18) A
The contents gives readers information about where to find
different sections of the text.

19) D
The text says that the word 'cuneiform' comes from the "shape of the
indentations" in the clay (line 20), which are made by the stylus.

20) D
The text says that readers enjoy the poem's "themes of friendship, life and
death" (lines 35-36), and that these themes are "relevant" (line 36) to
readers.

21) C
The text says that cuneiform was deciphered "in the 1800s" (line 41)
— this is the 19th century AD.

22) A
The text says that there aren't many people who can read cuneiform,
because it takes "years of study" (lines 44-45). As a result, many tablets
"have still not been studied" (line 47).

23) curators
The text says that "The task of preserving cuneiform writing
has now fallen to curators in museums." (line 44)

24) reed
The text says that a stylus would usually be "cut from a reed" (lines 18-19).

25) malleable
"malleable" (line 17) has the closest meaning to 'soft'.

26)   many of the tablets are damaged
"many of the tablets are damaged" (lines 28-29) is the
reason given for the poem not being complete.

27)   become, travel, dies
These are the three verbs in this sentence.

28)   adjectives
"distant" (line 5), "distinctive" (line 20), "ferocious" (line 32) and
"eternal" (line 34) are adjectives — they all describe nouns.

Maths — Main Test

Pages 13-20

29)   E — 1.6 m
1.25 m is 0.25 m away from 1.5 m, 1.7 m is 0.2 m away
from 1.5 m, 166 cm = 1.66 m is 0.16 m away from 1.5 m,
1490 cm = 14.9 m is 13.4 m away from 1.5 m,
1.6 m is 0.1 m away from 1.5 m.
0.1 m is the smallest distance away from 1.5 m, so 1.6 m is closest.

30)   B — 157
There are 43 + 114 = 157 people at the beach altogether.

31)   B — 2
There is one vertical line of symmetry
and one horizontal line of symmetry.

32)   A — Sci-fi
The most popular type of book has the biggest sector on the
pie chart. The biggest sector is for sci-fi, so the answer is A.

33)   C — 11 portions
1 kg = 1000 g, so the total amount of rice is
0.55 kg = 0.55 × 1000 = 550 g.
Divide the total amount by the amount in one portion:
550 ÷ 50 = 11 portions.

34)   D — 117
The fourth number is $(33 \times 2) - 5 = 66 - 5 = 61$.
The fifth number is $(61 \times 2) - 5 = 122 - 5 = 117$.

35)   C — 22
$a + 8 = 30$, so $a = 30 - 8 = 22$.

36)   B — £15.84
Eoin's total change is £2 + £2 + 10p + 5p + 1p = £4.16.
So his groceries cost £20 − £4.16 = £15.84.

37)   D — 0.4
4 out of the 10 sections are shaded. $^{4}/_{10}$ as a decimal is 0.4.

38)   C — 36 m
The perimeter of the whole garden is 12 + 12 + 7.5 + 7.5 = 39 m.
Leaving gaps for the gates: 39 − 1.5 − 1.5 = 36 m of fence.

39)   D — £32
Round the prices to numbers that are easier to work with:
1 box of paper ≈ £20, 1 roll of tape ≈ £1.50 and
1 pair of scissors ≈ £7.50. So a good estimate for the cost
of Theo's items is £20 + (3 × £1.50) + £7.50 = £32.

40)   B — 20 °C
The temperature at 5 pm is 27 °C.
There are 7 half-hours between 5 pm and 8:30 pm.
So the temperature at 8:30 pm is 27 − (7 × 1) = 20 °C.

41)   C — Yasmina, by 12 ml
Leyla has 226 + 215 = 441 ml of drink.
453 − 441 = 12 ml. So Yasmina has 12 ml more than Leyla.

42)   D — $^{5}/_{8}$
Ahmed has already played 3 of the 8 games, so there are
8 − 3 = 5 games that he hasn't played. The probability he
chooses a game he hasn't already played is 5 out of 8, or $^{5}/_{8}$.

43)   A — 55
The range is the difference between the lowest value and the highest value.
42 is the smallest number of pieces collected and 97 is the largest, so the
range is 97 − 42 = 55 pieces of rubbish.

44)   D — 9:47 am
Tracey snoozes for 4 × 10 = 40 minutes. When the alarm goes off
for the fifth time, she stays in bed for another 12 minutes.
So she gets up 40 + 12 = 52 minutes after 8:55 am,
which is 9:47 am.

45)   C — 1600 cm³
Volume = 5 × 8 × 40 = 1600 cm³

46)   A — 3
10% of 30 is 3, so 30% of 30 = 3 × 3 = 9.
There are 6 tally marks in the pop row so far,
so Kofi needs to add 3 more tally marks.

47)   D — (5, 5)
Only option D produces an isosceles triangle. Option A produces a
horizontal line and options B, C and E produce scalene triangles.

48)   E — 10%
19:54 is 9 minutes after 19:45, so he misses 9 minutes of
the match. $^{9}/_{90} = ^{1}/_{10}$, which is equivalent to 10%.

49)   C — 50p
2 paddles cost £6, so 1 paddle costs £6 ÷ 2 = £3.
So 4 ping pong balls cost £5 − £3 = £2.
So 1 ping pong ball costs £2 ÷ 4 = 50p.

50)   C — Othello
Woofer scored (2 × 4) + 2 + 2 = 12 points.
Spot scored (2 × 3) + 3 + 5 = 14 points.
Othello scored (2 × 5) + 2 + 3 = 15 points.
Joker scored (2 × 4) + 4 + 1 = 13 points.
Angel scored (2 × 2) + 5 + 5 = 14 points.
Othello scored the most points, so won the competition.

51)   12 mints
$^{1}/_{5}$ of 30 = 30 ÷ 5 = 6, so Oliver eats 6 mints.
He has 30 − 6 = 24 mints left to share equally.
Ruaridh gets half of 24 mints: 24 ÷ 2 = 12 mints.

52)   12°
180° − 47° − 121° = 12°.

53)   28 minutes
The next bus from The Inn after 16:30 is 16:47. It arrives at The Hill
at 16:55. Russell then walks for 3 minutes to get home, so he arrives
home at 16:58. This is 58 − 30 = 28 minutes after leaving work.

54)   44 pear trees
Subtract the number of all the other trees from the total:
120 − 30 − 18 − 28 = 44 pear trees.

55)   24 cm²
There are 21 full squares, and 6 half squares = 3 full squares.
21 + 3 = 24 squares, which is equivalent to 24 cm².

56)   61.2 cm
Difference in height: 16 hands − 10 hands = 6 hands.
6 hands = 6 × 10.2 = 61.2 cm.

Set A: Paper 2

English — Practice Test

Pages 2-3

P1) C
'house's' should be 'houses' — you don't add an apostrophe
to make something plural.

P2) C
'on' is correct because it completes the phrase 'on purpose'.

P3) A
'Unfortunatly' should be 'Unfortunately'.

P4) E
The text says that the tower was "built to be one of the main
attractions at the Paris World's Fair in 1889" (lines 1-2).

P5) fascinating
"fascinating" (line 7) means the same as 'interesting'.

Maths — Practice Test

Pages 4-5

P6) B — Cap
If Zahra received £2.10 in change, the item she bought must have
cost £10 − £2.10 = £7.90. The item that costs £7.90 is a cap.

P7) E — 10
Each symbol represents 4 trees. There are 4 symbols for birch,
so there are 4 × 4 = 16 birch trees. There are $1\frac{1}{2}$ symbols
for sycamore, so there are 4 + 2 = 6 sycamore trees.
So there are 16 − 6 = 10 more birch trees than sycamore trees.

P8) C — 249
287 and 256 both round up to 300. 345 and 329 both round down
to 300. 249 would round down to 200, so the answer is C.

P9) 1.1 m
Charlie is 105 + 5 = 110 cm tall. 1 m = 100 cm,
so Charlie's height in m is 110 ÷ 100 = 1.1 m.

P10) 70%
$\frac{35}{50}$ is the same as $\frac{70}{100}$, which is 70%.

English — Main Test

Pages 6-12

1) B
There should be speech marks before 'I think' to mark
the beginning of Gauri's speech.

2) C
There should be a second dash after 'damson' to separate the extra
information in the sentence ('strawberry and damson').

3) N
There are no mistakes in this line.

4) B
The semicolon between 'stage' and 'Reuben' is incorrect —
it should be a comma, as commas are needed when there is
a subordinate clause at the start of a sentence.

5) A
There should be a question mark between 'ruler' and the
inverted commas because Maisy is asking a question.

6) B
'they've' is correct because it is a contraction of 'they have',
which is consistent with the tense of the rest of the sentence.

7) E
'stood' is correct because it is the past tense form of 'stand',
which is consistent with the tense of the rest of the sentence.

8) A
'deeper' is correct — it is the only adverb that makes sense
with the rest of the sentence.

9) B
'moose' is correct — the phrase 'group of' needs a plural noun,
and 'moose' is the only option that can be a plural.

10) E
'enough' is correct — it is the only determiner
that makes sense in this sentence.

11) B
'assistent' should be 'assistant'. The suffix is 'ant', not 'ent'.

12) A
'blosom' should be 'blossom'. The word is spelt with a double 's'.

13) D
'larva' should be 'lava' — 'larva' means 'a young insect'.

14) N
There are no mistakes in this line.

15) C
'sensable' should be 'sensible'. The suffix is 'ible', not 'able'.

16) E
The device used is a simile — it compares the noise to a firework
using "as" (line 11).

17) B
Teeth chattering and pulling a coat tighter around yourself
are both signs of being cold.

18) B
The text says that the trees are "scratching" at the characters and
compares the twigs to "talons" (line 31). These unpleasant images
suggest the forest is an unwelcoming and hostile place.

19) D
"neither hide nor hair" (line 36) means 'no trace of something'.
If the characters have seen "neither hide nor hair" of the giant,
then they have not found any evidence that he is real.

20) A
The text says that the narrator's "mood lightened" (line 40),
which is another way of saying that they feel more positive.

21) E
The text says that the narrator "was sure he was about to roar"
(line 46), implying that they were expecting the giant to scare them
rather than talk to them.

22) C
The text says that the giant "likes privacy" (line 20), and that the
characters become friends with him, so it makes the most sense
that they would respect the giant wanting to remain hidden.

23) 15
The text says the meeting time is "7 o'clock" (line 9), but the narrator
arrives at "quarter past seven" (line 13), so they are 15 minutes late.

24) diary
Cara said she found her grandpa's diary (line 19) and that
was where she found the information about the giant.

25) illuminated
"illuminated" (line 27) means the same as 'lit up'.

26) roused
"roused" (line 43) means the same as 'awakened'.

27) adverb
"guiltily" (line 3), "finally" (line 18), "testily" (line 24) and "overhead"
(line 42) are all adverbs because they describe verbs.

28) adjective
"looming" (line 43) is an adjective that describes the noun 'presence'.

10

Maths — Main Test

Pages 13-20

29)   E — 35
55 coffees were sold on Friday. 20 coffees were sold on Tuesday.
So 55 − 20 = 35 more coffees were sold on Friday than on Tuesday.

30)   B — 20
1 litre = 1000 ml, so Marissa can get 1000 ÷ 250 = 4 bowls
from 1 litre. So she can get 4 × 5 = 20 bowls from 5 litres.

31)   C — 60
x needs to be a multiple of both 12 and 5.
Out of the possible answers, only 60 (= 12 × 5) is a
multiple of both — the rest are multiples of 5 or 12 only.

32)   E — 1
Number of halloumi burgers = 9 × 3 = 27. Number of
beef burgers = 7 × 4 = 28. Difference = 28 − 27 = 1.

33)   D — £7.96
3 packets of chewing gum cost £0.68 × 3 = £2.04.
Corrina's change = £10 − £2.04 = £7.96.

34)   D — One quarter turn clockwise
Option A goes to SW. Option B goes to SW. Option C
goes to NW. Option D goes to SE. Option E goes to NW.
So the answer is D.

35)   A — Amr
In order of shortest to longest, the times are:
5:34, 5:42, 5:47, 5:50, 6:01.
The third shortest is 5:47, which is Amr's time.

36)   B — 10
First add 7 to 23: 23 + 7 = 30.
Then divide the result by 3: 30 ÷ 3 = 10.

37)   E — four 10p coins and twenty 2p coins
Option A = 84 × 1p = 84p
Option B = 43 × 2p = 86p
Option C = (3 × 20p) + (6 × 5p) = 60p + 30p = 90p
Option D = (1 × 50p) + (2 × 20p) = 50p + 40p = 90p
Option E = (4 × 10p) + (20 × 2p) = 40p + 40p = 80p
80p is the smallest amount, so the answer is E.

38)   C — 3.15 m
Add the oil drum's height to the height it was raised:
1.62 + 1.53 = 3.15 m

39)   D — $\frac{1}{3}$
The numerator and denominator of $\frac{12}{36}$ both divide by 12,
giving the fraction $\frac{1}{3}$.

40)   A — 60°
All the angles in an equilateral triangles are the same.
So x = 180° ÷ 3 = 60°.

41)   E — Act IV
Act I lasts from 8:00 to 8:25, so is 25 minutes long.
Act II lasts from 8:25 to 8:45, so is 20 minutes long.
The interval lasts from 8:45 to 9:00, so is 15 minutes long.
Act III lasts from 9:00 to 9:20, so is 20 minutes long.
Act IV lasts from 9:20 to 10:05, so is 45 minutes long.
So Act IV is the longest.

42)   C — 8
The mean score is the total score divided by the number of scores.
Mean score = (7 + 8 + 7 + 9 + 9 + 8.5 + 7.5) ÷ 7 = 56 ÷ 7 = 8

43)   C — $\frac{2}{8}$
$\frac{2}{8} = \frac{1}{4}$ which is equivalent to 25%, not 40%.
All of the other fractions are equivalent to 40%.

44)   E — 95 cm³
The tin is a quarter full of beans, so the volume of beans is a
quarter of the volume of the tin: 380 ÷ 4 = 95 cm³.

45)   B — 36, 45
The difference between each pair of numbers increases by 1
each time. To get from 1 to 3 you add 2. To get from 3 to 6
you add 3. To get from 6 to 10 you add 4, and so on.
To get from 21 to 28, you add 7, so to get to the next two numbers
you need to add 8, then 9. 28 + 8 = 36, and 36 + 9 = 45,
so the next two numbers are 36 and 45.

46)   D — 21 °C
Find the difference between 3 °C and -18 °C:
From -18 °C to 0 °C is 18 °C. From 0 °C to 3 °C is 3 °C.
So the temperature rose by 18 + 3 = 21 °C.

47)   E — 55 ÷ 5
27 − 15 = 12, 32, 14 and 9 × 1 = 9 are all not prime.
55 ÷ 5 = 11, which is prime, so the answer is E.

48)   B — 5 faces, 5 vertices, 8 edges
A square-based pyramid has 1 square face and 4 triangular faces,
so 1 + 4 = 5 faces in total. It has 5 vertices and 8 edges,
as shown in the diagram below.

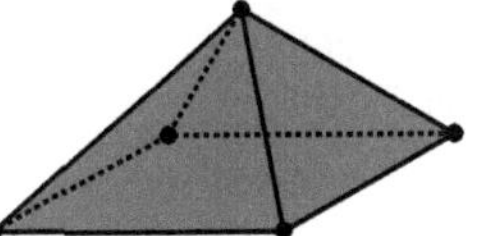

49)   C — $\frac{1}{6}$
The total number of chocolates = 11 + 4 + 3 + 5 + 7 = 30.
Probability of taking a hazelnut chocolate = $\frac{5}{30} = \frac{1}{6}$.

50)   C — £6
Penny's items cost £6.50 + £1.50 = £8.
25% of £8 = £8 ÷ 4 = £2. So Penny spends £8 − £2 = £6.

51)   328 g
20 ÷ 5 = 4, so you need to multiply the amount of flour needed
for 5 cookies by 4 to get the amount of flour needed for 20:
82 × 4 = 328 g.

52)   2 hours 10 minutes
The journey time between Otmel and Barbham is found by
looking at the time in the 'Otmel' row and the 'Barbham' column.
2:10 = 2 hours and 10 minutes.

53)   14.4 m²
Area of parking bay = 6 × 2.4 = 14.4 m²

54)   7 kg
At 5 months, the cross on the graph is on the line halfway between
6 kg and 8 kg, which is 7 kg.

55)   88 mm
The pentagons are regular and all the same size, so each side is 8 mm
long. The outside of the shape is made up of 11 sides of the pentagons,
so the perimeter is 11 × 8 = 88 mm.

56)   5 cupcakes
54 ÷ 7 = 7 remainder 5, so there are 5 cupcakes left over.

Set B: Paper 1

English — Practice Test

Pages 2-3

P1)   B
The colon between 'hamsters' and 'Jonathan' is incorrect —
it should be a semicolon. Colons should only be used to
introduce lists or explanations.

P2)   C
'because' is correct — it is the only conjunction
that makes sense in this sentence.

P3)   C
'apointment' should be 'appointment'.
The word is spelt with a double 'p'.

P4)   D
After Sita enters the apartment in line 5, she puts the container
"on top of the living-room table" (lines 5-6).

P5)   timid
"timid" (line 10) means the same as 'nervous'.

Maths — Practice Test

Pages 4-5

P6)   D — 70p
Tariq has 50 + 50 + 10 + 10 + 10 = 130p. £2 = 200p,
so Matilda has 200p − 130p = 70p more than Tariq.

P7)   D — Red
The colour that there were fewest cars of is represented by
the smallest sector on the pie chart. The smallest sector is red,
so there were fewest red cars.

P8)   E — 6
Regular polygons have the same number of lines of symmetry as
the number of sides. A regular hexagon has 6 sides, so it has
6 lines of symmetry as shown in the diagram below.

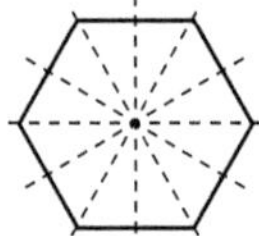

P9)   1.6 m
Josie climbed 5.5 m and Thibaut climbed 3.9 m.
So Josie climbed 5.5 − 3.9 = 1.6 m higher than Thibaut.

P10) 180 people
There are 3 × 20 = 60 people on the minibuses and 2 × 60 = 120
people on the coaches, so there are 60 + 120 = 180 people in total.

English — Main Test

Pages 6-12

1)   D
There should be speech marks after the question mark
to show the end of Timothy's speech.

2)   N
There are no mistakes in this line.

3)   A
The open bracket should start before 'who', as 'who was very confused'
is the extra information.

4)   C
The semicolon should be a colon as it is introducing a list.

5)   A
'could'nt' should be 'couldn't' — 'couldn't' is a contraction of 'could not'.

6)   C
'unless' is the only conjunction that makes sense in this sentence.

7)   D
'you'll' is correct — it is the only option that makes sense in this sentence.

8)   D
'cacti' is correct — the phrase 'a selection of' needs a plural noun,
and 'cacti' is the only option that can be a plural.

9)   A
'were walking' is correct — it is the only option that is consistent
with the tense of the rest of the sentence.

10) B
'fastest' is the only superlative adjective that makes sense in this sentence.

11) B
'apologysed' should be 'apologised' — the 'y' is changed to an 'i'
when the suffix 'ise' is added.

12) C
'recomend' should be 'recommend'.
The word is spelt with a double 'm'.

13) B
'past' should be 'passed' — 'past' means 'at an earlier time'.

14) N
There are no mistakes in this line.

15) D
'appearence' should be 'appearance'. The suffix is 'ance', not 'ence'.

16) E
"familiar to anyone even vaguely interested" (line 1) means that the
reader wouldn't need to know very much about space travel to have
heard of those names.

17) E
The text says that "the threat of men being sent to war prompted
an expansion of the team" (lines 12-13), which suggests that men
leaving for war would cause a staff shortage.

18) D
The text says that black women "were made to use segregated dining and
bathroom facilities" (line 18). This means statements 3 and 5 are true.

19) E
This statement tells you that Johnson's work was important to the NACA.

20) B
The text says "her trajectory calculations" (line 28) helped to make the
1969 moon landing successful.

21) B
The text says that Margot Lee Shetterly's book was published in 2016,
then says that the film came out "later that year" (line 46).

22) D
The text says that Margot Lee Shetterly's book details "the lives and
achievements" (line 46) of West Computers such as Johnson, Vaughan
and Jackson to the public.

23)   National Advisory Committee for Aeronautics
The acronym is written out in line 10.

24)   Katherine Johnson
The text says that Katherine Johnson was "awarded...the
Presidential Medal of Freedom" (lines 43-44) in 2015.

25)   expansion
"expansion" (line 13) means the same as 'increase'.

26)   the tide has begun to turn
"the tide has begun to turn" (line 43) is another way of saying
'things are starting to change'.

27)   think, travelled, do, constitute
These are the four verbs in this sentence.

28)   adverbs
"less" (line 16), "accidentally" (line 23), "most" (line 33) and "relatively"
(line 41) are all adverbs because they all describe verbs or adjectives.

Maths — Main Test

Pages 13-20

29)   C — 25 s
The range is the difference between the slowest and fastest times.
Rahul was the slowest, with a time of 59 s.
Maeve was the fastest, with a time of 34 s.
So the range is 59 − 34 = 25 s.

30)   D — It has two pairs of equal-length sides.
A rectangle has two lines of symmetry, not four, so A is not true.
A rectangle always has four right angles, so B and C are not true.
A rectangle has four sides, two short sides of the same length and
two longer sides of the same length, so D is true and E is not.
So the answer is D.

31)   C — 15:33
Mr O'Brein left his house at 14:35. He spent 14 minutes driving
to the shops, 28 minutes shopping, and 16 minutes getting home.
So he spent 14 + 28 + 16 = 58 minutes away from home.
So he arrived back at home 58 minutes after 14:35, which is 15:33.

32)   B — $^{1}/_{3}$
30% = 0.3, $^{3}/_{10}$ = 0.3, $^{30}/_{100}$ = $^{3}/_{10}$ = 0.3, so 30%, $^{3}/_{10}$, 0.3
and $^{30}/_{100}$ are all equivalent. $^{1}/_{3}$ is equivalent to 33.3...% or 0.333...,
so $^{1}/_{3}$ is not equivalent to the others.

33)   E — Triangular prism
Shape z has more than 5 vertices and at least 1 triangular face.
A cylinder has 0 vertices and 0 triangular faces.
A cuboid has 8 vertices and 0 triangular faces.
A square-based pyramid has 5 vertices and 4 triangular faces.
A cone has 1 vertex and 0 triangular faces.
A triangular prism has 6 vertices and 2 triangular faces.
So a triangular prism is the only option with more than 5 vertices
and at least 1 triangular face. So the answer is E.

34)   B — 1 hour and 12 minutes
96 ÷ 8 = 12, so it takes the machine 12 lots of 6 minutes to make
96 boxes. 12 × 6 = 72 minutes. There are 60 minutes in
an hour, so 72 minutes is equivalent to 1 hour and 12 minutes.

35)   A — £5.14
10 apples cost 10 × 36p = 360p = £3.60. 6 bananas cost
6 × 21p = 126p = £1.26. So Devi spends £3.60 + £1.26 = £4.86.
So Devi gets £10 − £4.86 = £5.14 change.

36)   B — $^{3}/_{10}$
There are 8 + 4 + 10 + 6 + 12 = 40 T-shirts and 12 of them are
white. So $^{12}/_{40}$ of the T-shirts are white. 12 and 40 both divide by 4,
so $^{12}/_{40}$ can be simplified to $^{3}/_{10}$.

37)   A — 30
Each small division on the vertical axis of the chart represents
2 children, so there are 18 children who have been to the cinema
0 times and 12 children who have been to the cinema once.
So there are 18 + 12 = 30 children who have been to the cinema
fewer than two times in the last year.

38)   B — 162
The rule for the sequence is 'multiply the previous number by 3'.
The last number given in the sequence is 54, and 54 × 3 = 162.

39)   E — 25 km
Maisden and Westpool are 5 cm apart on the map.
The scale is 1 cm = 5 km, so 5 cm on the map is
equivalent to 5 × 5 = 25 km in real life.

40)   D — 56
When a number is multiplied by itself, the result is a square number.
100 = 10 × 10, 36 = 6 × 6, 49 = 7 × 7, 121 = 11 × 11.
56 is not a square number because there is no number
that you can multiply by itself to make 56.

41)   E — (11, 7)

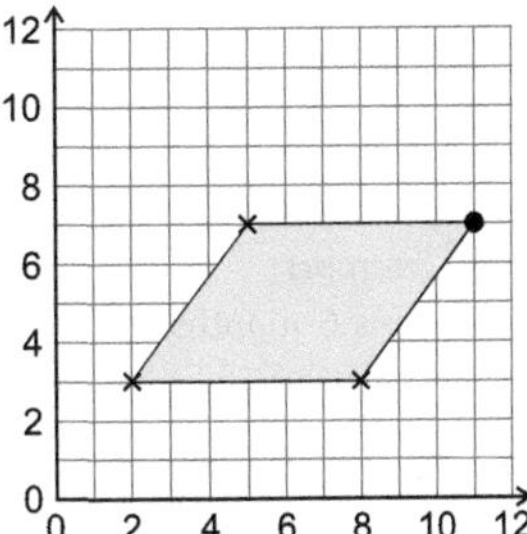

The completed parallelogram is shown on the grid above.
The fourth point is marked with a dot and has coordinates (11, 7).

42)   A — 1 kg
The mass of 1 bag of flour is 4.5 kg ÷ 3 = 1.5 kg. The mass of
1 bag of sugar is 2500 g ÷ 5 = 500 g. 500 g is the same
as 0.5 kg, so the difference in mass between one bag of flour and
one bag of sugar is 1.5 kg − 0.5 kg = 1 kg.

43)   D — 1:15
Liana fell asleep at 5:05 pm and woke up at 6:20 pm.
There is 1 hour and 15 minutes between 5:05 pm and 6:20 pm.

44)   C — 3002
To multiply 30.02 by 100, move the decimal point 2 places to the right.
So 30.02 × 100 = 3002.

45)   B — 85%
There are 12 red pens and the rest are black, so there are
80 − 12 = 68 black pens. So the probability that Arlo
chooses a black pen is $^{68}/_{80}$ = $^{17}/_{20}$ = $^{85}/_{100}$ = 85%.

46)   A — 46
There are 10 full symbols, which represent 10 × 4 = 40 records.
There is one quarter of a symbol worth 1 record, one half of a symbol
worth 2 records, and three quarters of a symbol worth 3 records.
So in total there are 40 + 1 + 2 + 3 = 46 records.

47)   D — 56
7 × 8 = 56, so 7 and 8 are both factors of 56. 42 and 84 have 7
as a factor, but not 8. 64 and 72 have 8 as a factor, but not 7.

48)   A — Prisha, by 1 cm
Raj has grown by 7 cm = 0.07 m. His new height is 1.23 + 0.07 = 1.3 m.
Prisha has grown by 7 × 2 = 14 cm = 0.14 m.
Her new height is 1.17 + 0.14 = 1.31 m. 1.31 − 1.3 = 0.01 m = 1 cm,
so Prisha is 1 cm taller than Raj.

49)   C — £28.50
Over 16 weeks, Zena receives £2.50 × 16 = £40. She spends £11.50
on a bracelet, so she has £40 − £11.50 = £28.50 left.

50)   B — 4750 g
Each small division on the scale is 0.25 kg. The arrow on the scale
is pointing at three divisions above 4 kg, which is 4.75 kg.
4.75 kg × 1000 = 4750 g.

51)   12 cm²
Use the lengths given to work out the sides of the shaded rectangle.
One side is 10 − 6 = 4 cm and the other side is 5 − 2 = 3 cm.
So the area of the shaded rectangle is 4 cm × 3 cm = 12 cm².

52)   7 minutes 30 seconds
The small divisions on the thermometer are 5 °C, so the arrow is pointing
at 110 °C. This means the sugar needs to be heated by a further 50 °C.
This will take 5 × 30 = 150 seconds. 1 minute = 60 seconds,
so 150 seconds = 2 minutes and 30 seconds. So Fionn heats the sugar
for 5 minutes + 2 minutes + 30 seconds = 7 minutes 30 seconds in total.

53)   £1.50
Shauna buys 3 museum tickets for £45, so 1 museum ticket costs
£45 ÷ 3 = £15. Bridget buys 1 museum ticket and 6 souvenir postcards
for £24. 6 souvenir postcards cost £24 − £15 = £9.
So 1 souvenir postcard costs £9 ÷ 6 = £1.50.

54)   424 g
Isla needs 400 + 340 = 740 g of clay. She has
114 + 97 + 105 = 316 g. So she needs 740 – 316 = 424 g
more clay to make the plant pot and saucer.

55)   6 months
January, February, March, April, November and December
all have average temperatures less than 11 °C, which is 6 months.

56)   244 cm
The bridge is 8 bricks high, so it is 8 × 30.5 cm tall. 30.5 splits
into 30 and 0.5. 30 × 8 = 240 cm and 0.5 × 8 = 4 cm.
So the bridge is 240 + 4 = 244 cm tall.

Set B: Paper 2

English — Practice Test

Pages 2-3

P1)   D
There shouldn't be a comma after 'and'.

P2)   A
'the' is correct — it is the only determiner
that makes sense in this sentence.

P3)   B
'shreik' should be 'shriek'. The spelling rule is 'i' before 'e', except after 'c',
as long as the word rhymes with 'bee'.

P4)   E
The text says women did the "majority" of the household chores (line 7)
and that Haslett wanted to let them know how "electricity could make
their lives easier" (line 8).

P5)   revolutionise
"revolutionise" (line 7) means the same as 'transform'.

Maths — Practice Test

Pages 4-5

P6)   B — 2:45
The time on the clock is 2:30. 15 minutes later will be 2:45.

P7)   C — 150 g
The scale is showing 350 g. Zach had a 500 g bag of flour,
so if 350 g is left, he used 500 – 350 = 150 g.

P8)   B — $^3/_5$
Aisling has 20 – 8 = 12 sheep on her farm, so $^{12}/_{20}$
of her animals are sheep. Simplifying this fraction gives $^3/_5$,
so the answer is B.

P9)   5 Labradors
All the names within the Labrador circle, including the overlap,
need to be counted. The names in the Labrador circle are
Barney, Lulu, Smartie, Bella and Indy, which is 5 in total.

P10) 20 children
25% of 80 = 80 ÷ 4 = 20, so 20 children play football.

English — Main Test

Pages 6-11

1)   B
There should be a comma rather than a full stop after 'food', as
commas are needed when there is a subordinate clause at the start of
a sentence.

2)   C
The question mark should be an exclamation mark,
as 'What a beautiful day it is' is an exclamation.

3)   B
'its' should be 'it's' — 'it's' is a contraction of 'it is'.

4)   N
There are no mistakes in this line.

5)   B
There is no need for a comma after 'immediately'.

6)   E
'so' is correct — it is the only conjunction that makes sense
in this sentence.

7)   A
'practised' is correct — it is the only option that is consistent
with the tense of the rest of the sentence.

8)   B
'my' is correct — it is the only possessive determiner
that makes sense in this sentence.

9)   D
'tallest' is correct — a superlative adjective is needed
to complete this sentence.

10)   E
'who' is correct — it is the only relative pronoun
that makes sense in this sentence.

11)   B
'substence' should be 'substance'. The ending is 'ance' not 'ence'.

12)   N
There are no mistakes in this line.

13)   C
'relevent' should be 'relevant'. The ending is 'ant' not 'ent'.

14)   D
'altar' should be 'alter'. 'alter' means 'to adjust', whereas an 'altar'
is a holy table in a religious building.

15)   D
'insufferible' should be 'insufferable'. The suffix is 'able' not 'ible'.

16)   D
The second and fourth lines of each stanza rhyme,
for example "skies" and "demise" (lines 2-4).

17)   A
The speaker says "I felt my heart lift" (line 9),
which implies that they feel hopeful.

18)   B
Exclamation marks are often used to show excitement or strong feelings.
In this context, the speaker is showing excitement about the plant's
growth.

19)   E
The speaker watched the plant grow "For many weeks" (line 21), which
means that they observed the plant growing slowly. It also says that the
speaker decides to "tend" the seedlings (line 28), which means the speaker
started looking after them. This means statements 3 and 5 are correct.

20)   D
The metaphor suggests that the insects' wings must be very colourful,
like mosaics.

21)   C
The speaker says they give the visitors things "To make themselves a
thriving spot" (line 44), which means that they want the visitors to make
their own gardens.

22)   D
The speaker says that their garden is "The only place not burnt and dried"
(line 39), which suggests that the speaker doesn't think there
are any other gardens in the world.

23) 2 (or two)
The text says that the plant has "one small pair" (line 10) of leaves to start with.

24) wind
The text says that the screen was built to "shield" (line 13) the plant from "harsh winds" (line 14).

25) tentatively
"tentatively" (line 22) means the same as 'hesitantly'.

26) far and wide
"far and wide" (line 37) means the same as 'many places'.

27) preposition
"in" (line 2), "on" (line 15), "Despite" (line 24) and "from" (line 29) are all being used as prepositions in the poem.

28) verb
In this text, "gift" (line 43) is being used as a verb.

Maths — Main Test

Pages 12-20

29) B — 84 cm
Noah jumped $4.62 - 3.78 = 0.84$ m further than Olajide.
Convert to cm: 0.84 m $\times 100 = 84$ cm.

30) B — 38
Maggie buys $5 \times 6 = 30$ small glasses,
and $3 \times 4 = 12$ large glasses.
So she buys $30 + 12 = 42$ glasses in total.
She throws away 4, so Maggie has $42 - 4 = 38$ glasses left.

31) D — 22
The percentage of members whose favourite paint is oil is:
$100\% - 26\% - 30\% = 44\%$
44% of $100 = 44$, so 44% of $50 = 44 \div 2 = 22$.

32) A — The arrow lands on 1.
The sector for 1 has the smallest area,
so the arrow is least likely to land on it.

33) C — 27p
Caoimhe has £9.97 + £12.76 = £22.73 in total.
So she needs £23 − £22.73 = £0.27 = 27p more.

34) C — 21:47
10:02 pm is 22:02 in twenty-four hour clock time.
Fifteen minutes before 22:02 is 21:47.

35) B — 0.16
$\frac{4}{25} = \frac{16}{100}$, which is 0.16 as a decimal.

36) E — V and Y are perpendicular.
Y and Z aren't parallel because they cross each other. V and X aren't parallel because they cross each other. Z and X aren't perpendicular because they aren't at right angles to each other. X and Y are parallel to each other, so D isn't true. V and Y are perpendicular because they are at right angles to each other, so the answer is E.

37) B — 3.8 kg
$380 \times 10 = 3800$ g, which is $3800 \div 1000 = 3.8$ kg.

38) A — 75%
50% of $64 = 32$, so there are 32 black squares.
Motsi paints 16 more squares black,
so there are now $32 + 16 = 48$ black squares.
$\frac{48}{64} = \frac{3}{4}$, which is equivalent to 75%.

39) E — 18 cm
The longer side of the rectangle is 2×3 cm $= 6$ cm.
So the perimeter is $3 + 6 + 3 + 6 = 18$ cm.

40) D — 12:12
The train should leave Olby at 11:57, but it is
$6 + 9 = 15$ minutes late. So it leaves Olby at 12:12.

41) E — $\frac{1}{6}$
There are $4 + 7 + 9 + 4 = 24$ children in total.
4 children scored 16-20. So the fraction is $\frac{4}{24} = \frac{1}{6}$.

42) C — £1.40
3 packets of crumpets cost £4.20, so 1 packet of crumpets costs £4.20 ÷ 3 = £1.40.

43) E — 33
Pattern 1 contains 2 triangles + 1 square = 3 shapes.
Pattern 2 contains 6 triangles + 2 squares = 8 shapes.
Pattern 3 contains 10 triangles + 3 squares = 13 shapes.
So each pattern gains 4 triangles + 1 square = 5 more shapes.
Pattern 7 is 4 steps more than Pattern 3, so it will have
$4 \times 5 = 20$ more shapes than Pattern 3, which is 33 shapes.

44) B — 30
The mean score is the total score divided by the number of players.
The total is $18 + 37 + 40 + 25 + 30 = 150$ and there are 5 players.
So the mean is $150 \div 5 = 30$.

45) D — 48
There are $60 \div 5 = 12$ cracked pieces of pottery.
So there are $60 - 12 = 48$ undamaged pieces of pottery.

46) B — Week 4
Week 4 is plotted at a height of 11 cm on the graph,
but it should be at 12 cm to match the table.

47) E — isosceles triangle
Acute angles are less than 90°. The scalene and right-angled triangles each have 2 acute angles. The square and the pentagon have no acute angles. The isosceles triangle has 3 acute angles, so the answer is E.

48) E — (7, 6)
T is at (7, 4). It is reflected over the line $y = 5$. Since its y-coordinate is 1 square below 5, the reflected y-coordinate will be 1 square above 5, so at $5 + 1 = 6$. Its x-coordinate will not change, so the new coordinates are (7, 6).

49) C — £9
Four dining chairs normally cost £62.25 × 4. £62.25 = £60 + £2.25.
£60 × 4 = £240 and £2.25 × 4 = £9. So £62.25 × 4 = £249,
which is £9 more than £240, so the offer saves £9.

50) A — 18 °C
Half of 66 °C is $66 \div 2 = 33$ °C.
$33 - 15 = 18$ °C, so he serves the cake at 18 °C.

51) 30°
The two missing angles add up to $180° - 120° = 60°$.
The triangle is isosceles, so both these angles are the same,
so $x = 60° \div 2 = 30°$.

52) 45 cm²
Total area $= 20 \times 12 = 240$ cm².
The area of the frame is the difference between the total area
and the area of the empty space, which is $240 - 195 = 45$ cm².

53) 450 seconds
There are $60 \times 7 = 420$ seconds in 7 minutes.
There are 30 seconds in half a minute.
So there are $420 + 30 = 450$ seconds in 7 and a half minutes.

54) 30%
There were 30 plays in total, 9 of which were rock.
$\frac{9}{30} = \frac{3}{10}$, which is equivalent to 30%.

55) 1.8 litres
Tomi uses $178 + 22 = 200$ ml of milk, and there are
2 litres = 2000 ml in the bottle. So after the milk is poured,
there are $2000 - 200 = 1800$ ml of milk left in the bottle.
So there are $1800 \div 1000 = 1.8$ litres of milk left in the bottle.

56) 48 cm³
There are 6 cubes in the shape, and each one has a volume of 8 cm³.
So the volume of the shape is $6 \times 8 = 48$ cm³.